THE
UNITED COUNTIES
STORY

THE
UNITED COUNTIES
STORY

ROBERT COOK & ANDREW SHOULER

TEMPUS

First published 2006

Tempus Publishing Limited
The Mill, Brimscombe Port,
Stroud, Gloucestershire, GL5 2QG
www.tempus-publishing.com

British Library Cataloguing in Publication Data.
A catalogue record for this book is available from the British Library.

ISBN 0 7524 3199 4

Typesetting and origination by Tempus Publishing Limited
Printed in Great Britain

CONTENTS

ACKNOWLEDGEMENTS

The authors would like to thank everyone who kindly provided photographs and time to talk of their experiences. The book owes its origins to Derek George and the Stoke Goldington archive. Derek introduced the authors to each other some years ago and they have since collaborated on a number of projects. Particular thanks are due to, Duncan Allen, R.J. Bell, Gavin Booth, Ron Bull, N.G. Cook, Nicola Cook, Mrs P. Croy, George Crutchley, Brian Dale, Eric Edwards, Mrs Ruth Eyre, Ray Fall, Derek George, Tom Goodwin, Mrs E. Harris, Sue Harris, Alan Henshall, Bucks Herald, W.J. Hill, W.G. Horwood, Julian Hunt, Barry Keane, Bill Kirby, Phillip Lamb, Graham Ledger, Graham Mabbutt, Keith Martin, Olive Martin, Bill Meredith, M.K. Metro, Alan Millar, Irene Mortimer, Vauxhall Motors, Ron Naylor, Fred Newman, Northampton Borough Council, *Northampton Chronicle & Echo*, Dave O'Dell, R.U. Palmer, John Payne, Baden Powell, John F. Pratt, A.J. Reed, Sir Bob Reid, Jim Royle, Dawn Rush, Jeremy Seabrook, Dave Shelley, R.H.G. Simpson, Colin Stacey, George Tasker, Maurice Tasker, Colin Harvey Taylor, Des Tunks, Colin W. Wardle, Roger Warwick, A. Warwick, Bob Wesley, Gordon White, Bert Woodfield. There are many others who have contributed to the formation of the authors' bus interest over the years, not least of whom are the people who ran the buses that they have so much enjoyed travelling on. Every effort has been made to trace photograph copyright holders.

INTRODUCTION

This book is concerned with the history and development of bus and coach services in an area approximately corresponding to that covered by the largest and most influential company: United Counties (UCOC), now part of Stagecoach East. From its headquarters in Northampton, its sphere of influence once extended from Stamford and Market Harborough in the north, down to Oxford, Aylesbury and Luton in the South and from Daventry in the west to Bedford and Cambridge in the east. There was an additional service to Cambridge, following the demise of the Oxford–Cambridge railway link, and a service from Cambridge to Bedford. United Counties thus covered most of the south-east Midlands.

An abbreviation of 'omnibus', the Oxford English dictionary defines the noun 'bus' as 'a road vehicle plying on a fixed route and open to all comers'. The word has worldwide use, although the vehicle itself was the invention of seventeenth-century French mathematician Blaise Pascal. He and his colleagues ran a short-lived bus service in Paris during the early 1660s.

Although the full expression 'omnibus' was incorporated into company names, like the UCOC, the full term was seldom used. The prefix omni means 'every', or 'all' and was, in large part, a means of travel for the unwashed masses. Working folk were not going to mess about with fancy long words when there was no need. In more recent years, as mass motoring has changed life styles, relying on the bus in Britain tends to attract a certain social stigma, except in our most congested cities.

The revolution has been most obvious in the old United Counties area of Milton Keynes. This was once an area of wide-open spaces and rolling pastures stretching from North Bucks into Bedfordshire, but in the late 1960s the region was being transformed into the land of the motor car. This was against the will of its original planner, County Architect Fred Pooley, who wanted a monorail city. Milton Keynes was re-designed and built with car ownership in mind. Land was cheap and the vision was of compact estates and large green spaces. Old fashioned double- and single-deck buses would never get around them, even if there were customers waiting. Ironically, however, millions was spent on a marble bus station, which Andrew Shouler has likened to Lenin's mausoleum.

Open day at Winterhill, May 1984, and newly repainted and overhauled Bristol VR 798 stands proud. Note the spruce-looking engines to the left. Although the Milton Keynes allocation still awaited their City Bus logo, this wide expanse of white paint in the livery was a one off. (Andrew Shouler)

An open day, 19 May 1984, at UCOC'S new depot at Winterhill, Milton Keynes. The four vehicles are all ex-UCOC but withdrawn and owned by enthusiasts. Just peeping out from behind the Lodekka (second from right) is a then-current Leyland/Willowbrook V-registered coach. The site is now a Home Base furniture store. (Andrew Shouler)

Lots of oil stains the ground in this summer view of Milton Keynes bus station in 1984. Although showing Aylesbury allocation plates, this Leyland National displays the City Bus logo. Milton Keynes depot was notorious for not painting the plates. Milton Keynes was supposed to be black on green and Aylesbury red on blue. (Andrew Shouler)

The fact remains that the Development Corporation's grand plan to integrate bus and rail travel stations on the west side of Milton Keynes failed and the great windswept bus station edifice became far more popular with skateboarders than bus boarders. The location sees little bus traffic and is earmarked for redevelopment. A bus garage facility built for the United Counties Bus Co., combining the two United Counties depots at Bletchley and Stony Stratford, Winterhill was far too grand a scheme in an age and place of declining bus travel.

Deregulation saw a variety of operators using the depot, most significantly the major local successor to United Counties, MK Metro. At the time of writing, Julian Peddle's MK Metro is being taken over by Arriva. This is an interesting development considering that Stagecoach sold the MK business to Julian Peddle and he sold his Rhondda enterprise to them. It would have pleased some of us UCOC enthusiasts if there were a chance of a reversion to Stagecoach.

However, Milton Keynes, with all its suburbs named after the once leafy little villages they were built upon, no longer has the lanes for rattling UCOC buses to roll along or the people who are inclined to use them. As Milton Keynes Council's transport cabinet member, Graham Mabbutt told us that it is too easy for people to drive from one side of the city to the other for them to be bothered with buses. Problems arise though when people are trying to get in and out of the place in peak times.

When the Government's intention to double the size of Milton Keynes by 2031 was announced, Milton Keynes Council commissioned a study to look into ways of

Winterhill, Milton Keynes, Open Day 1984. VR number 959 displays its complicated inner workings. Note the bodywork panels displayed around it and the open pit. Goodness knows how many barriers would be required under 2006 Health and Safety legislation. Common sense still played a part twenty-two years ago. (Andrew Shouler)

A Bristol L type number 426 single-decker rambles along twisting lanes between Northampton and Gayton in the early 1960s. (John Royle)

quadrupling public transport use from 4 per cent of all internal journeys to 16 per cent. Graham Mabbutt, interviewed in summer 2004, said that it would be very difficult to reach this goal over the next thirty years of the expansion programme. As Milton Keynes Transport Cabinet member, he said in an interview with Robert Cook that only parking charges and bus lanes would help a modal shift back to buses, adding that it was optimistic to expect to achieve quadrupling of bus passengers, to 16 per cent by 2031, when the second phase of Milton Keynes expansion will have been completed.

The man in charge of Milton Keynes expansion, Sir Bob Reid, said in interview: 'To get public transport going it has to be reliable, frequent, easy to use and relatively affordable. London has done this with a much larger population, by giving the residents travel permits which are taken up in money paid in rates… One of the great faults of traffic designers is that they take people where they don't want to go.' (*Not A Two Speed City* – Robert Cook 2006).

Milton Keynes has been attractive to the affluent London over spill and a booming service economy. Further north in the old UCOC area, around Wellingborough, there is not so much prosperity and United Counties, subsumed under the Stagecoach East banner, are doing rather better. This was an area hit by the economic policies of the Thatcher years, which destroyed the British steel industry. Cars here are less commonplace and the highways less conducive to easy driving.

Some say widespread availability of motor cars, through cheap credit and the second-hand car market has helped make everyone middle class. This is a point of view with which the authors would not agree. In late Victorian and early Edwardian times class distinctions were more clear-cut. While the working classes used trams and third-class railway carriages, middle-class folk took horses and early motor buses into leafy suburbs, way beyond the limiting infrastructure of steel rails.

Tramcars were a variation on railways, with New York having led the way in 1831. The idea soon spread Europe-wide. The Wolverton–Stony Stratford service opened in 1887, with spur to Deanshanger, featuring huge cars with a carrying capacity up to 120 and pulled by German-built locomotives. This service was used mainly by men travelling to work at the London & North Western Railway (LNWR) works in Wolverton. The

MK Metro Bus enters the old village of Shenley Brook End, now a suburb of Milton Keynes, in 2004. This former North Bucks countryside was part of the old United Counties running area. (Robert Cook)

The Wolverton & Stony Stratford Steam Tramway opened on 27 May 1887 and ran on a 3ft 6in gauge roadside track for nearly 2.75 miles between the towns – there was a short lived 2 mile extension to the village of Deanshanger. The LNWR eventually took over the tramway. Here we see engine number 5, a Bagnall saddle tank with skirts fitted to contain motion and avoid frightening horses. It has set out from Stony Stratford, heading east to Wolverton and towing two large 100-seater trailers. The tramway closed in May 1926, as a result of the General Strike of that month. (Martin Blane)

Wolverton & Stony Stratford Tramways Co. was formed in November 1882. The daily fare was 1s a week, which was a sizeable chunk out of a weekly wage of 25s. Yet with boots at 7s a pair, it was still cheaper than walking. Company takings soon topped £45 a week. The tramway came under the control of the LNWR in 1920, closing six years later as a consequence of the General Strike. Peterborough, Northampton and Luton also invested in tramways, but although Bedford and Wellingborough gained permission, the Acts of Parliament were allowed to lapse with no systems being built. This left a void in Wellingborough that would be filled by the precursor of United Counties.

Of course a past of rumbling, swaying, clanking trams, bustling buses and chirpy cloth-capped workers is too easily sentimentalised. On the other hand the present too easily venerated, because political correctness and vested interests will not allow fair criticism. Yet for those of us who can remember, much has been lost. Some idea of this is gleaned from a United Counties Tours handbook of the early 1960s:

> United Counties Omnibus Company Ltd, whose registered offices are at Houghton Road, Northampton, operate regular Stage Carriage Services throughout practically the whole of the counties of Buckingham, Cambridge, Hertford, Huntingdon, Leicester, Lincoln, Oxford and Rutland, the outlying towns served being Amersham, Aylesbury, Oxford, Buckingham, Daventry, Leicester, Oakham, Stamford, Peterborough, Ramsey, Cambridge, Buntinford, Letchworth, Luton and Tring.
>
> A regular daily express service is operated between Nottingham and London, via Leicester, and Northampton, and then either via the motorway or Dunstable and St Albans. Express services operated with our associated companies to all parts of the country, also run throughout the year. During the summer months there are direct services to Skegness, Yarmouth, Lowestoft, Clacton, Jaywick Sands, Margate, Ramsgate, Portsmouth and Southsea, Bournemouth, Brighton, Hastings and Eastbourne.
>
> The Northamptonshire countryside is typically English in character, of a serene and gracious type of beauty, without notable ranges of hills, yet well wooded and well tilled, with an infinite variety of scenery. Many of its villages and localities figure in the history of England, and its churches are unequalled for their magnificence – indeed, Northamptonshire has been called the county of 'spires and squires'.
>
> Bedfordshire, unlike its neighbour Northamptonshire, does in its south-western corner have some famous hills – the Chilterns, locally known as Dunstable Downs. Picturesque beauty abounds in the county. There are fragrant pine woods and sandy hills on the Buckinghamshire border and also the beautiful Whipsnade Zoo, where animals are kept in a comparatively natural environment. John Bunyan, who wrote *Pilgrims Progress*, is very closely associated with the county and many noteworthy places of interest are to be found in 'the Bunyan country'.

Of course not all the beautiful countryside has been lost, but it has been diminished and the pace of life rather quickened. Thus, no modern bus company would take time to dwell on matters of outlook or the landscape upon which they travelled, particularly through means of such an elaborate, illustrated and substantial timetable publication.

Leyland TS7, with Eastern coachwork, number 403, seating thirty passengers, standing at Gloucester Green bus station in Oxford to work to Victoria via High Wycombe and Uxbridge – in spite of its roof board reading Nottingham, Leicester, Norhampton, St Albans, London! New in 1935, it was withdrawn in 1951. (R.H.G. Simpson)

One of the UCOC's illustrious Bristol REs, number 253, pictured in the mid-1960s having just arrived at Nottingham, via the M1 motorway. Its good looks were further enhanced by the cream band being continued under and around the windscreen (R.H.G. Simpson)

What would there be to describe apart from endlessly similar estates, shopping centres and traffic jams?

Also gone is the company that provided so much service under one company roof, working in harmony with many other businesses that made up our once great National Bus Co. Still we must not denigrate the achievements of the successor company, Stagecoach, who have taken over part of the old United Counties operations. At least they have retained the fleet name and are making a go of it in difficult times and the vehicles still carry legal lettering of United Counties Omnibus Co. Ltd. The brother–sister partnership of Brian Souter and Ann Gloag, from humble beginnings, has done much to keep a large part of the British bus industry running in the challenging age of the motor car.

The Souters epitomise the power of enterprise, though some of their ambitions have not always been fulfilled and on the international stage they have been very ambitious. That is in the nature of events and it is the way it all began. Energy crises, demographic change and road congestion may well force us back on to the motor bus and even trolley buses have a chance. Sir Bob Reid argues, in the case of Milton Keynes:

> Equally it is clear as people get older they will be less able or keen to drive themselves. This has two implications, one they'll want the services they need…Close to home…By design you are reducing dependence on the motor car and increasing reliance on public transport.

Sir Bob says he is no fan of trams:

> They are alright in places like Melbourne where there is one very long street. They would not suit Milton Keynes.

A new age of bus travel may be upon us, but not along the winding country lanes that many idealise and some remember. With the current pace of change and centralisation of Government we may soon witness the demise of our counties and there may be none to unite. At the same time much of the old UCOC countryside is to be concreted over by order of Deputy Prime Minister Prescott's office. We cannot go back in this life and we can only wonder what is to come.

Robert Cook & Andrew Shouler
May 2006

1

ON THE MOVE

Ever since humans stood upon two legs they have felt the urge to move around, initially only to obtain food, water and shelter. Eventually tracks evolved and traces of two such ancient ways can be found in the region covered in this account. In the south, the Icknield Way on the scarp slope of the Chiltern Hills passes north-east of Ivinghoe and Dunstable to Norfolk; in the north the Jurassic Way progresses from the Cotswolds north-eastward through the Northamptonshire Uplands to the Lincolnshire Wolds.

Innovative Romans realised the importance of well-maintained roads for the successful operation of their far-flung empire, thus creating the Watling Street, heading north-west from London to North Wales, a route much used by coaches and buses over the years. The Romans' departure led to neglect and it declined into a muddy track, although royal parties en route to Northampton Castle kept the way open. Civil War in the seventeenth century provided a further boost. Not until more settled times could private carriages be developed. The seventeenth century saw the emergence of the Hackney carriages and stagecoach services were well developed by the nineteenth century.

Stagecoaches enabled those who could afford it to travel much further afield, with services to a set timetable over pre-advertised routes, offering opportunities for travel between London and the provinces. Journeys were still time-consuming and difficult, but it was a considerable improvement on the earlier slow and cumbersome stage wagons where passengers had to sit among loads of goods and chattels. One such stage wagon was advertised in the *Northampton Mercury*, 22 July 1782, as leaving the town at 2 a.m. on Wednesdays and Fridays, arriving in London at 4 a.m. on Thursdays and Saturdays – a journey of twenty-six hours for some 66 miles. This vehicle was grandly named the *Flying Wagon*. Allowing for stopping time to change horses, pick up and set down goods, it averaged 3mph!

Considering the parlous state of roads and the whims of weather, such speed might be thought of as flying. Turnpike Trusts charged tolls. These monies funded road improvements early in the eighteenth century. Innovator Thomas Telford was one of those employed to realign and re-grade existing roads, doing a lot of work on the Watling Street – nowadays called the A5. Mail was carried along these routes in specially designed and built Royal Mail coaches, travelling at an incredible 6mph. Routes from

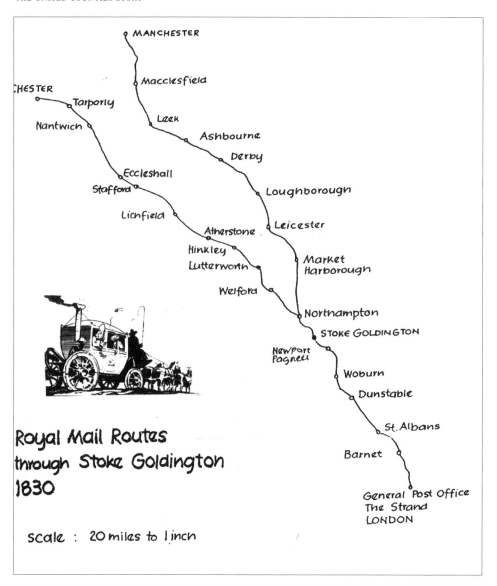

MANCHESTER

Macclesfield

CHESTER
Tarporly
Leek
Nantwich
Ashbourne
Derby
Eccleshall
Stafford
Loughborough
Lichfield
Leicester
Atherstone
Hinkley
Lutterworth
Market Harborough
Welford
Northampton
STOKE GOLDINGTON
Newport Pagnell
Woburn
Dunstable
St. Albans
Barnet
General Post Office
The Strand
LONDON

Royal Mail Routes through Stoke Goldington 1830

scale : 20 miles to 1 inch

London, the Midlands and the North passed through the area from Peterborough in the east (the present A1), Luton, Bedford and Kettering (A6), Northampton (A50), Dunstable–Towcester (A5) and Aylesbury (A41). In 1830, five coaches travelled daily through Northampton bound for Manchester, including the Royal Mail at 3 a.m., having left the Post Office in the Strand at 8 p.m. the previous evening, travelling via St Albans, Dunstable, Woburn and Newport Pagnell.

In addition to these long-distance progenitors of National Express, there were local coaches starting from regional market towns, most bound for London but a variety going across country. Destinations included Cambridge and Northampton. These routes are extant nearly 200 years later.

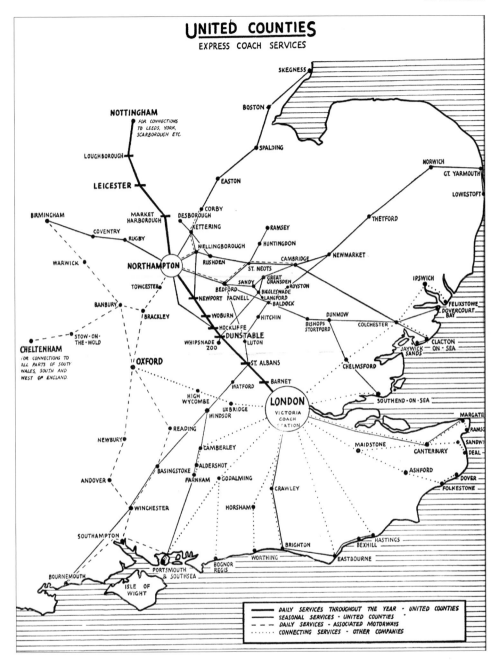

Above: United Counties Express Service Routes, March 1953; the influence of early stagecoach routes is noticeable. (Colin Harvey Taylor)

Opposite: Royal Mail Stagecoach routes through Stoke Goldington, 1830. (Andrew Shouler)

Birch Brothers Bus Garage, café and offices brought art deco to Rushden, Northants in 1937. Note the 'Café Airflow', a reference to the streamlining craze epitomised by the Chrysler Airflow car. Birch were required to relinquish London routes and from the mid-1930s developed various services in Herts and Beds plus a long-distance route from Kings Cross to Rushden via busy RAF Henlow camp and Bedford. Being so busy with servicemen, Birch used double-deckers. Birch sold out to United Counties in 1969, for £48,500. (Authors' collection)

Local coaches were organised and financed by local people, often local merchants and inn keepers who had a vested interest as their premises served as staging posts. These coaches generated local patronage, travellers preferring to use the local town coach rather than that of a long distance competitor. Yet the settled situation of stagecoach travel was devastated by the opening, in 1838, of the London–Birmingham railway, providing competition on the London services that no coaching organisation could resist. Rail travel was quicker and cheaper; steam power far outstripped the mighty horse. Once main lines were complete, the branches filled in the gaps and stagecoaches were doomed by the 1850s.

Various Acts of Parliament, concerned to protect road services, prevented steam power from taking over road travel. An infamous Act of 1865 limited mechanical vehicles to 4mph and insisted that a man with a red flag walked ahead to warn approaching horse traffic. Railway companies, however, saw the potential of something similar to a stagecoach for the purpose of ferrying passengers and luggage to stations.

The concept of the bus was first demonstrated in Britain in 1829 by George Shillibeer. He operated a horse-drawn passenger vehicle from Paddington Green in West London eastward along Marylebone and Euston Roads, on through Islington and down to the Bank. The single-deck vehicle featured a rear door into a van body with perimeter

A Midland Motor Omnibus Co.'s Thornycroft double-decker waits outside the Dolphin Public House on Newport Pagnell's Markey Hill to work to Bedford. Note the horse trough by the sign. In 2006 both the Dolphin and the attractive Georgian house remain, but the fine trees have long since been felled. The tall chimney of the Phoenix Brewery towers over the scene. (Julian Hunt/ Dennis Mynard)

seating. This was something quite different to stagecoaches. The service departed Paddington at 9 a.m., noon, 3 p.m., 6 p.m. and 8 p.m. The 1s fare was hefty for those days but the example inspired other London and Provincial city services.

Horse buses were a natural development of the stagecoach as the Industrial Revolution created poverty, urban sprawl and a flight of the better off to the suburbs. Elizabeth Birch was the enterprising widow of a London Horse cab operator. William Birch operated stage and mail services in the West Country, long before railways turned the tide of transport technology. Railways changed the family fortunes and his son went to London to run cabs from Horseferry Road. Elizabeth started her own bus service from Mansion House to Pimlico in 1847. She died in 1874 and her two sons went on trading independently until they formed Birch Brothers Ltd, in November 1899.

The Red Flag Act was repealed in 1896, with the maximum speed increased to a startling 12mph. Motor bus services grew apace. Locally, Sir Walter Carlile of Gayhurst House had been an early motor enthusiast, being the first MP to arrive at the House of Commons in his own motor car. Thus he supported a local twelve-seater service from Newport Pagnell to Olney.

Petrol engines were becoming increasingly reliable and were preferable to steam. The stage was being set for the emergence of the UCOC. The National Bus Co. of which

A busy Kingsbury Square, Aylesbury, in the early 1930s, with several local buses including a Red Rover with white painted tyre walls. The four staff members discussing matters in the centre look perilously close to the saloon coach's rear. Both car and bus carry London registration plates. Passengers could buy fruit and confectionery for their journeys from the surrounding shops. (Authors' Collection)

it became a part had origins dating back to Thomas Tilling's horse-bus service which grew rapidly from 1847, becoming a public company in 1897, with 4,000 horses used to haul its vehicles.

Tilling ran the company's first motor bus in 1904. BET followed suit through their British Automobile Traction Company Ltd (BAT), but Tilling's growth was frustrated by the London General Omnibus monopoly and had to look beyond London, becoming involved with BET. The First World War stimulated motor vehicle design and construction, with a fleet of London B-type buses shipped to France as troop carriers. Maintenance and driving skills became widespread, feeding back into civilian life, and a plethora of regional bus companies were developed. Some of these enterprises would attract the interest of the combined Tilling & British Automobile Traction Co. Ltd (TBAT), formed in May 1928. TBAT was effectively a holding company for the two groups. Those were days of cut throat competitions, with London General Omnibus Co. (LGOC) the major contender for London's Transport requirements. The company went into the doldrums and gave up altogether in 1912 – resuming bus services after the First World War. Tillings, LGOC and Road Car were the only three companies with any stability on the London bus scene. Skills in both the driving and maintenance of motor buses were scarce and in their infancy.

The London Passenger Transport Board (LPTB) took them all over in 1934. However, Birch had by then developed express services outside the LTPB area. During these

United Counties fleet number C8, a Leyland GH7 with a body built by UCOC themselves, seating sixty. This bus was new in April 1924 and sold in December 1931. It is photographed on Abington Square prior to working service 2 eastwards to Wellinborough. The service was later extended through to Finedon and Irthlingborough. Note the conductor's polished leather leggings and commodious cap. The Draper's shop premises behind the bus later became UCOC's office and waiting room. (Authors' Collection)

pioneering days, Wellingborough in mid-Northamptonshire had benefited from a Saturday afternoon and evening service by a moonlighting crew normally employed by the London Central Motor Omnibus Co., using a bus belonging to their employer who was unaware of this profitable sideline. The company were not pleased and the men left to form the Wellingborough Motor Bus Co. in May 1913.

This company blossomed into the United Counties Road Transport Co. on 1 September 1921. The United Counties Omnibus & Road Transport Co. began life as a private company on 1 September 1921. The assets of the Wellingborough Motor Omnibus Co., which it had replaced, included thirty-seven useable vehicles. The new company took over the Northampton Motor Omnibus Co. in 1928. Northampton had almost been the capital of England and was an ideal central location for the new company to base its operations. W.J. Hill recalled living on the A45 in 1920, just outside the Northampton town boundary, opposite the milestone to Wellingborough:

> The buses came past twice a day and three times on Wednesday market day, into town. They had solid tyres and no top and were run by the Irthlingborough Omnibus Co. United Counties took them over. They ran some services alongside Yorks, but Yorks were very occupied with coastal excursions. United Counties took over Alchins and many others, including Knights who did contract coaching. I think they took over Beedon's first. I remember Beedon's had an old charabanc.

United Counties favoured Leyland chassis during independent days. Here we see RP5007, fleet number 108, Leyland Lion carefully negotiating a flooded main road along the A6 in Nene Valley, between Irthlingborough and Rushden. Note the large number of insulators on the telephone posts, signifying an important trunk route. The bus had a Short's body, built under sub contract to Leyland. It seated thirty-five passengers, was new in 1927 and withdrawn in the late 1940s. (Authors' Collection)

The company became UCOC in 1933 when Thomas Tilling acquired it. Eastern National express services benefited, to some extent, from poor railway links to London in their operating area. Thomas Tilling Group had taken Eastern National over in 1931. Following the Tilling take-over, United Counties name was changed to the United Counties Omnibus Co. (UCOC).

Individual companies retained something of their own identities, although most favoured Leyland or AEC vehicles. The latter originated as an in-house chassis and engine supplier for London General Omnibus. AEC was eventually taken over by Leyland and wound up in the 1980s. Bristol was another great bus builder and a name intimately associated with the National Bus Co. Sadly it would experience the same fate as AEC, disappearing through a Leyland takeover.

Significantly the British Electric Traction Company (BET), formed in 1896 to exploit electric motors for transport, was soon offering services over a wide area, including much of industrial England and Wales. The Peterborough Electric Tramway was running fourteen trams by 1901, adding routes to Dogsthorpe, Newark and the showground, with their centre terminus at Long Causeway. They ran their first double-deckers by the mid-1920s.

The 1924 Road Traffic and London Traffic Acts helped and encouraged independent operators and express coach services were being established. Red Rover started life in

Late in its UCOC life span (note the pneumatic tyres), Leyland RAF type S6 was photographed on Campbell's Square, Northampton. New in June 1921, it passed to a Manchester operator in December 1929. Whilst the conductor wears full uniform complete with leather faced cuffs, the burly driver has to be content with just a cap. (Authors' Collection)

London, using Daimlers. London Transport originated through a nationalising scheme of 1933. This brought order to a world of pirate buses. Formation of the London Passenger Transport Board robbed Red Rover of its express Aylesbury to London services – a route choice based on the fact that E.M. Cain, one of the company's two brothers who had founded Red Rover, had an aunt living there. Without this route, Cain turned his attention to Aylesbury-based local routes, rivalling United Counties on the Aylesbury to Buckingham run. His business had started life on London services 14 and 49 in 1924. His business was compulsorily taken over by the London Passenger Transport Board in 1934.

Northampton commenced horse-drawn tramway operation in 1881 and the Northampton Street Tramways Co. was taken over by the corporation in 1901, being electrified in 1904. By 1914 there were nearly 6.5 route miles. Although a cross-town trolleybus link with the tramways was authorised in 1911, it was never built and corporation buses replaced trams in 1934. Luton commenced electric tram operation in 1908. Luton Council owned 5.25 route miles with services operated by a private company, running thirteen trams. The council took over the business in 1923, buses replacing trams in 1932. The pre-war fleet were mainly Daimlers, after 1945 they were various.

In the 1920s and early '30s, many roads were little better than cart tracks, following the meandering path of a hundred tinkers wending their way through unspoilt countryside. W.J. Hill said:

Corporation tram in Gold Street, Northampton, c.1910. Trams were replaced by more adaptable buses by the 1930s. De-regulation in the 1980s saw the corporation system pass to First Bus. (Authors' Collection)

Luton's tramway opened in 1908 and one of the corporation fleet is seen here, George Street, c.1908. Luton's earliest motor buses belonged to Road Motors, starting with services to Hitchin, Dunstable and St Albans. Road sold out to the National Bus Co., which later became linked to United Counties. Controversially, the council wanted to sell its transport rights in 1931, but the Government wouldn't let it. United Counties would acquire the council fleet in the early 1970s and the lot would be hived off by profit-crazed Thatcherite Tories. (Authors' Collection)

A Wesley-owned Gifford bus of the Bluebell fleet at Olney in the early 1930s. (Derek George)

In the 1920s it was difficult riding any distance on a solid tyred bus, sitting on slatted wooden bench seats. The country roads were sand and gravel at best and it didn't get better until you got into Northampton at Abington Park. The buses did about 18mph, which was fast.

An interesting picture of those olden days is painted by Mrs E. Harris of Northampton. Now ninety years old, she recalls:

When I was a young girl in the 1920s, the United Counties Bus Depot was in small square in Horsehoe St, running off from a cross roads, which was not a very good plan. It lay at the back of the Shakespeare Public House on the corner of Marefair. Later on it moved to St Giles Street in the town centre. I used to go there regularly for Dovers Ltd, the firm I worked for, as van driver. I worked for them for 27 years. They made motor and cycle accessories. One of their products was number plates. For a small fee, I took them to be collected, at nominated bus times, for village garages, where the buses dropped them off. It was cheaper than sending me with the van. My elder sister worked as a conductress during the war years on United Counties.

In the early days, United Counties favoured Leylands, while smaller operators rumbling along the same roads had a motley selection of vehicles. Wesleys brought the famous Ford Model T on to the local scene. These charming little forerunners of today's giant luxury coaches plied their way daily between Newport Pagnell and Northampton. Times changed, and so did the vehicles. Wesleys were proud when they took possession

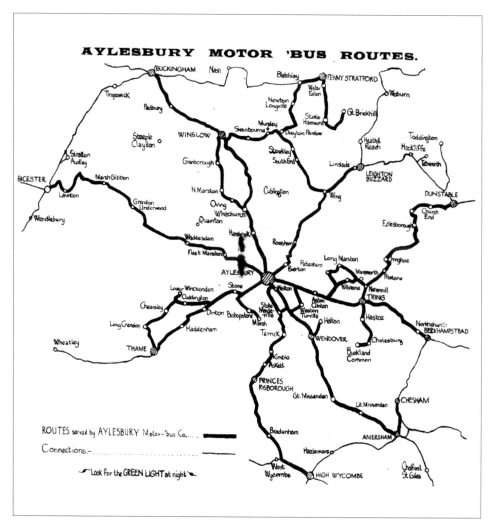

This 1930s map demonstrates that 'Aylesbury Motor Bus' were a thriving independent covering a lot of route miles. This made them a target for Tilling's Eastern National, extending their routes into north and mid-Bucks.

of a De Dion Bouton twenty-four-seater – one of the most advanced touring coaches of the day – built on long low lines with a heater and a radio. Passengers would not enjoy the same luxury on a United Counties service bus, but their vehicles were among the best available.

Bristol Tramways had begun motor bus operations in 1906, using twelve Thornycroft double-deckers. Their management was also involved with the aircraft manufacturing company at Filton, where they started building their own buses. Later they moved to Bath Road, Brislington. Two world wars saw the company forced to switch full-time production to aircraft components, but the 1930s were vital years when they developed vehicles particularly suited to passenger service.

Good reasons why **YOU** should support the

AYLESBURY
Motor 'Bus Co.

IN PREFERENCE TO OUTSIDERS.

WE ARE THE PIONEERS OF MOTOR BUS SERVICES IN THIS DISTRICT.

WE HAVE GIVEN YOU CONTINUOUS SERVICES FOR THE PAST 11 YEARS.

WE CONTRIBUTE SOME HUNDREDS OF POUNDS YEARLY TO LOCAL RATES — OUTSIDE COMPANIES DO NOT CONTRIBUTE A PENNY.

THE

Aylesbury Motor 'Bus Co.,

Proprietor: E. W. Young

The County Garages, Aylesbury.

This proclamation of the merits of Young's Aylesbury Bus, urging folk to travel by local carrier, would be counter-productive. Eastern National saw the success story and took them over, creating part of another Tilling subsidiary. UCOC took over these operations in 1952. (Authors' Collection)

During this period, the neighbouring Tilling company, Western National Omnibus, took over Bristol. Tilling already controlled Eastern Coach Works in Lowestoft. The Eastern Coach Works (ECW) built and put bodies on Bristol chassis. The Bristol ECW combination became the hallmark and main load bearer of the Tilling operation until the demise of the National Bus Co. in 1988.

2

TILLING EMPIRE

Under Tilling, the new company's operating area changed and expanded. Express services from Oxford to London were established, with an eye to the bright future of coach travel, as public works schemes promoted road improvements. Operations around Luton, Dunstable and Aylesbury were transferred to neighbouring Eastern National, which was also part of Tilling, in 1933. United Counties purchased Alchins in 1933 and there was a general clamour among operators to consolidate express services.

The need to co-ordinate services and obtain economies of scale led to the formation of Associated Motorways on 1 July 1934. The group comprised United Counties, Greyhound (including Bristol Tramways), Red & White, Black & White, and Midland Red. The member companies agreed to work together, offering their services as part of a whole business and focused on the Black & White's Cheltenham bus station which opened in 1932, where interconnection of services was facilitated.

The rise of the motor car was not unforeseen during the 1930s coach and bus heyday. Buckinghamshire County Council produced a 1931 structure plan full of road improvements, monster roundabouts and leaf-filled sketches of proposed suburban paradise. Road deaths were around 9,000 a year, mainly due to inadequate driver training and the primitive state of cars.

In those days bus timetables were often works of art, carrying adverts and little homilies. For October and November 1932, Amersham & District Motor Bus & Haulage Co. included 'The Road Code' which read:

Every road user should be acquainted with the Highway Code, published at the beginning of 1931. The code has not the force of law, but in proceedings under the Road Traffic Act, any failure to observe it may be taken into consideration. Its principal rules are: Never take a risk in the hope that everyone else will do what is necessary. Warn children of the dangers of the road and teach them how to avoid them. Walk on the footpath where there is one. If there is no footpath, walk on the right so as to face oncoming traffic. Regulate your speed to the circumstances and weather. Be ready to pull up within the distance which you can see to be clear. When stopping, slowing down or changing direction, give the proper signal clearly and in good time. Watch for traffic signs and signals. Never overtake unless you can

Driver Frank Johnson, in his white summer smock, poses with others at Maidwell, 10 miles out of Northampton and 7 miles from Market Harborough. His express coach is parked behind them, bearing route boards for Northampton–Market Harborough daily service in the early 1930s. (Dawn Rush)

see sufficiently far ahead to do so. When you do, give a warning beforehand. Do not cut in. Never accelerate when being overtaken, but keep to the left and signal the other driver on. Drivers on a minor road approaching a major road should go dead slow and give way to other traffic. Drive cautiously at crossroads and junctions. Do not stop your vehicle at awkward places – a bend in the road or congested thoroughfare – and do not stop at crossroads or by a point-duty constable to ask the way. If driving a slow moving vehicle, keep well to the left. Use your horn judiciously as a warning, not as a threat; but do not take it for granted that your warning has been heard.

The extract also included pictures of hand signals, because that was all they had in the early days. Cars were no more than boxes on wheels, with Austin, Morris and Ford providing for the lower end of the market. Car makers battled to keep cars cheap and ownership was a beacon of lower-middle-class aspiration. The Automobile Association had admitted its millionth member by 1930 and car ownership reached 2 million by 1939. War and petrol rationing eventually put this 'progress' on hold, but it also stimulated technical advance and improved mass production techniques.

Up until 1939, Britain had basked in the inter-war pleasures of a public transport system that was the envy of the world. London Transport, following in the wake of the Metropolitan Railway's achievements, cut deeper into the countryside, transforming much of South Buckinghamshire into suburbia. The inter-war years were hard times for many and bus driving was a job worth having. Nevertheless, many gambled their

Frank Johnson, posing by the garden gate, c.1930, in his smart driver's uniform. His family always exhorted him to take a job on the corporation buses and get a pension, but he loved his job on United Counties too much for that. (Dawn Rush)

livelihoods by joining the General Strike in 1926. However, the strike had little effect on busmen outside London.

United Counties busmen could consider themselves well off compared to many, but there were benefits to be had from joining a trade union. Crews employed by local authorities were easily organised, and those working for railway bus companies, like GWR, joined the National Union of Railwaymen. The situation with private provincial companies was more volatile. They tended to join the Transport and General Workers Union (TGWU). Bus personnel had to negotiate around national agreed standards of terms and conditions and the union did not always get always want to be involved in local disputes.

Before the Second World War, the company was serving hundreds of square miles and work schedules were demanding. Vehicle design made a quantum leap forward from 1925–30 through the introduction of pneumatic tyres, lightweight, high-speed chassis, better transmissions and brakes. The Associated Equipment Company (AEC) learned from its rivals that, to make best use of all the new arterial roads with their much faster surfaces, improvements were called for. Its new chief engineer, G.J. Rackham, re-joined the company in 1928 after twelve years working on tanks and in the USA, where he became chief engineer with the Yellow Coach Co. in 1922. Here, high-speed vehicle development for cross-continent travel was a necessity and well-advanced.

Returning to Britain to join Leyland and back to AEC, Rackham developed a range of passenger chassis, replacing old 4-cylinder power units with smooth-running 6-cylinder units. He placed a 6.1 litre engine in the Reliance Chassis, changing the designation from 426 to 660 and adding the company logo of inverted triangle with the London General bullseye and letters AEC on the bar. The maximum legal length was increased by 1ft to 26ft in 1930. An oil engine had already been tested in a 1928 works bus and an 8.1 litre direct injection unit was tested in a Regent double-decker. Power was increased to 8.8 litres in 1931 after trials with various operators. London and AEC were setting the standard.

As the bus and coach business boomed, so did the demand for drivers and thus, driving had to be made easier to recruit them. Daimler was using pre-selector gear boxes derived from Wilson patents. The fluid flywheel eased up on the gear changing and smoothed the ride and AEC gained permission to build them under licence. These advances were essential to widening the spread of public transport on the highway.

Eastern National took over the County Garages premises of E.W. Young who had operated his Aylesbury Bus Co. from there, Young had advertised himself as a pioneer of motor bus services, dating from 1917.

Among those observing these pioneering activities was young Ron Bull, living in Spratton, 6 miles north of Northampton. Like many he had become dependent on the modern bus service. He recalled: 'Before United Counties arrived on the scene, most of the villages were serviced by their own "bus privateers".' These would have been people like Mr Wesley and his Bluebell Coaches, from Stoke Goldington. The late Bob Wesley remembered his father taking payment in kind, taking commodities like cigarettes for his services. Bob and his brother Bill had other ideas and were among the smaller companies to survive alongside UCOC and the Tilling empire. Ron Bull's uncle, George Blundell, ran a bus from Spratton to Northampton. He said;

When United Counties appeared, they either bought routes from the existing operators or forced them off the road by a campaign of 'dirty tricks'. These consisted of either increasing the frequency of their timetables or undercutting the fares. Most of the privateers were ex-service drivers from World War One and they didn't have the financial means to contest them. So they went out of business and a lot of them were subsequently employed by United Counties as drivers.

In 1935, when I was 11 years old, I won a scholarship to Northampton Grammar School. This meant travelling to Northampton by bus. United Counties provided, mostly, a good service. The first bus was at 6am, then 7am and two at 8am, then 9am with services every two hours after that. Evening services from Northampton were around 4pm, two at 5pm, then 6pm, with the last one on weekdays at 10 pm (11pm on Saturdays).

The company also used to run two extra afternoon buses for visitors to the Creaton TB Hospital- the next village along the route on the old A50. The usual 'work-horse' was the Leyland single decker, a reliable petrol driven bone shaker. On the heavy passenger routes they used the heavy diesel engined Bristol double decker. Passengers could buy a weekly worker's ticket at a reduced fare and if you missed a day you could claim a refund at the Northampton office.

The bus garage and maintenance depot was at Bedford Road, Northampton and the bus station at Derngate, from and to which local town and county services departed and arrived. Long distance services also used Derngate – which included offices, restaurant and snack bar. I recall, when departure times were due, the station controller would blow his whistle and off the buses went. They left behind a nice mixture of petrol and diesel fumes, but we survived!

Around the late 1930s, the drivers and conductors went on strike. This became rather violent when the company shipped in 'scab drivers' from outside. This resolved in violent resentment with missiles being thrown at the buses along their routes. Chicken wire was placed over the windows to protect the passengers. We school boys initially took great delight in directing these drivers off their proper routes- thus making us late for school with a good excuse!

The unofficial strike that ensued was in January 1936. It was over the national agreement. In his *History of British Bus Services*, John Hibbs explains:

One of the effects of the Road Traffic Act was to stimulate the growth of trade union membership amongst busmen throughout the country. This coincided with the spread of combines for, in the words of H.A. Clegg, 'Many of the companies which were taken over were paternalistic, easy going little companies, and the newcomers introduced methods of rationalisation which were opposed by the men who turned in many cases for the first time to union organisation for protection'.

One of the United Counties strikers, Fred Marsh, produced a book, simply called *Busmen on Strike*. He described the struggle as a small affair, unorthodox in its conception and execution, but concluding that it made history on certain points. As far as Fred Marsh was concerned the strike was a culminating point of a series of changes in which workers, as usual, came off worst through conflict with the boss. The author noted that prior to absorption in the big combine, United Counties was purely a local undertaking, run on local capital, with many shareholders known to employees. He argued that many of these shareholders were frightened into selling their shares by certain of the directors who backed the Tilling take over and that, through an agent, the Tilling combine bought up shares as they came on the market. Once Tilling had control, the group set about rationalisation.

According to Fred Marsh, rationalisation meant: '…adding to the board of directors a number of unnecessary officials, all wearing their "old school ties", and cutting down the workers' wages to pay for it'. Marsh went on to attest that under the old regime employees had six days work a week and were paid on a daily basis. In addition to the regular staff, a number of men who had other jobs and were free on Saturday afternoons worked on the undertaking to supplement their weekly wage. 'These part-time men were now given the choice of leaving their other employment and taking a regular job on the buses or of losing their weekend jobs. This was the beginning of the plan to worsen our conditions.'

The majority of men accepted Tilling's conditions, replacing old pay rates and conditions which were as follows, as published by the United Counties' employees committee: A flat rate for drivers of 13s 6d per day: for conductors 11s 6d per day: all extra work above the usual day's work was paid for at 1s 5d per hour drivers, and 1s 3d per hour conductors. All work done on Saturday morning before 9 a.m. was paid for at these rates in addition to the day's pay. There was a six day week. A special bonus was paid during the holiday weeks to cover the extra work done. Christmas Day was paid for but not worked. A sick and dividend club existed to which all men paid a shilling per week and the company contributed an equal sum.

There were three grades of men, service men on regular duties, spare men who worked on the service men's rest days and weekends, thus getting a full week's work: and who probably had other jobs in other industries. All grades were on the full rate. The committee emphasised that any driver and conductor, working six days a week, could not earn less than £4 1s 0d and £3 9s 0d without any extra time or payments whatever.

Cutting working hours to five and one third days reduced wages by 9s and 7s 8d for drivers and conductors respectively. The sick and dividend club was scrapped, each man losing an annual share out at Christmas, averaging between £3 and £4. The holiday week bonus and the special bonus for early Saturday work was scrapped.

New employees were engaged at 2s a day less than the old stagers. They were promised two half yearly increases of 1s a day to bring them up to the regular rate, but the strikers were sceptical. United Counties' Busmen's Central Strike Committee published a leaflet, 'Busmen v Combines.' The document was issued by unions across the Tilling enterprises. It commented:

For some time past, considerable discontent has shown itself amongst busmen owing to the harsh conditions under which they work. Long and arduous hours of duty, irregular and insufficient meal times, long spread overs, low wages, speeding up of services are typical. It is not uncommon for a man to be up in the morning in time to report for duty at 5am and not to return home until 11 o'clock at night, involving total time away from home of 18 to 20 hours. If he is two minutes late reporting for duty, he is liable to be sent home or get a day's suspension at some future date as a penalty for reporting late to work.

These conditions have contributed to the cause of many strikes which might have been avoided had the Companies concerned been less intent on squeezing the maximum amount of profit out of the public and the men. It is not the desire of the employees to cause trouble, but this is their only weapon of hitting back when sprung upon.

The busman is expected to bear all the restrictions placed upon him without complaint. He suffers through the speeding up of schedules, bad meal breaks, personal responsibility for money losses or 'shorts', parcel deliveries, all for a small wage.

Busmen are expected to study the safety and interests of the public, but no regard is paid by employers to the fact that these men are ordinary human beings who require time to eat, sleep and enjoy leisure in order to maintain themselves in a fit condition.

The pamphlet described the steady increase in traffic and how conductors' duties were becoming steadily more arduous. The union accused the employers of ignoring all of this whilst expecting crews to remain alert and avoid accident, so as to safeguard and assist the 'bus riding' public. They felt they were being taken for granted. If they complied without protest, they felt that they would be pushed even further into slavery. They stated that there is a limit to human endurance, but that: '…the controlling interests of the British Electric Traction Company and Thomas Tilling… now control separately or jointly, the majority of the provincial bus undertakings in this country'. Busmen saw Tilling as simply being out to gain a monopoly to make big profits, driving out or taking over any smaller firms in their way.

There can be no doubt that Tilling had no need of parsimony. Dividends increased by £11,000 over three years between September 1933 and September 1935, as the following table affirms:

Year Ending	Gross Profits	To Depreciation & Reserves	Dividends to Shareholders
September 1933	£58,108	£33,009	£12,500
September 1934	£60,520	£33,746	£19,057
September 1935	£63,085	£34,034	£23,500

The Committee spelt out, in no uncertain terms, how the new owners were exploiting the workers:

On January 24th 1934, the company presented £35,000 in ordinary shares to the shareholders as a bonus. Of this amount £23,901 went to Messrs Tillings. This £35,000 came out of the 'To depreciation and Reserves' and so when the company plead that they didn't make £63,000 profit last year, we can well ask, 'how much of the £34,000 allotted to depreciation and reserves is actual profit and will be presented to the shareholders as bonus in the future?' Last year £3,500 was paid to the shareholders as interest on these bonus shares for which they had paid not a penny. At the same time, the Company converted all the 8% shares into Ordinary shares on which 10% has been paid since 1922. As a result, this year they paid an extra £2,500 to the owners of these shares without any costs to the lucky recipients.

But this is only half the story. On March 20th, 1934, the Company proceeded to issue £65,000 worth of ordinary shares to the shareholders at the rate of £1 for each £1 share. When Messrs. Tillings bought the United Counties Bus Company, they paid holders of £1 ordinary shares 38s 6d per share so that in effect, the issuing of 365,000 worth of ordinary shares to the shareholders at the rate of £1 for each £1 share (par). When Messrs Tillings bought United Counties Bus Company, they paid holders of £1 ordinary shares at par instead of at least 35 shillings per share, put a minimum of 348,750 in capital appreciation into the pockets of shareholders of which Messrs Tilling's received 95%. Last year 36,500 was paid in interest on these shares. If the money had been raised at 35 shillings per £1 share (this is a conservative estimate) only £3,714 would have been paid out in interest on them, a saving of £2,786 per year.

Thus we find that out of the additional £11,000 paid to the holders of Ordinary shares last year (1934), over £8,786 was given to shareholders as a free gift and will be given to them every year as long as the company pays a 10% dividend on the Ordinary shares.

The company's nominal capital in 1933 was £150,000, paying a dividend of £12,500. Two years later the capital was £250,000, paying £23,500. The employees committee argued that the company were hiding a real rise in average rate of dividend from 8.5 per cent to 12.5 per cent, an increase of 50 per cent. They took the view that if there was going to be any share out on this grand scale, they were entitled to have their standards safeguarded.

The public were asked to help by bringing all possible pressure to bear on the company to give the men a square deal. They suggested postcards, letters and resolutions of protest to the company from all organisations . The committee also made resolutions to the Traffic Commissioner, protesting against excessive speed, unreasonable services and unsatisfactory travelling facilities.

The intending strikers believed that with fair publicity the travelling public would support them. This drive for a united front of provincial busmen was reported in the *Daily Telegraph*. The report mentioned an unconstitutional committee representative of the men of seven companies in the Tilling B.E.T Group. The committee sat for over six hours and the main point under discussion was the co-ordination of the employees of the various companies to form a united front. A committee delegate told the *Telegraph*: 'It is hoped that by outlining a series of demands, which will be uniform, as a guide to the employees in their aim to achieve satisfactory wage standards and conditions, that success will ultimately be achieved in this direction'. He was rather optimistic.

Finances were centralised under Tilling and old ways had to be abandoned. Fred Marsh wrote:

> The speeding up of routes was the next part of the plan, and this was carried out to such an extent that not only were we asked to do impossible speeds, but the running cards were so packed with extra mileage that we were doing six days' work and sometimes more in five days.
>
> For years before the change over in ownership we had a very good club into which we paid one shilling per week and the company paid one shilling per week per man. This covered us for sick pay and at Christmas each year the balance was shared out amongst the members. The share out amounted to between £2 10 s and £3 each. Now the club was scrapped.
>
> Things went from bad to worse and firmer concessions were filched away from us one after another, each new move of the company leaving us just a little bit worse off.
>
> In December, 1934, we could stand it no longer and made our first real effort to stem the tide by threatening a withdrawal of labour. The company immediately loosened up a little and probably someone caught it in the neck for not being subtle enough grinding us down.

Strength of feeling on both sides made conflict inevitable. The 1930s were tough times and bosses guarded their profits as much as they could. Part-timers who had given up other work for full-time bus jobs were made redundant. Though the working week was cut to five and one third days, other concessions had been lost. In Fred Marsh's words:

> We now called in the Union officials and threatened strike action for Union recognition. Our membership at this time was 95 per cent. The company agreed to meet the Union officials, who after protracted negotiations, came to us with an offer of one shilling and a half penny for conductors. This on an eight hour day meant a reduction of four shillings and two pence per day for drivers and three shillings and two pence for conductors on our recognised daily rate. To set against this reduction, we were offered a guaranteed week of forty eight hours and six days' holiday a year with pay, while the old hands would have in addition a bonus of four shillings a week.

On Saturday morning, 4 January 1936, battle commenced at Irthlingborough, organised by a small nucleus and word spread by strategic use of activists in cars and on motorcycles. The fitters joined the struggle. Fred Marsh reported:

> The first bus had left Northampton depot as usual but was caught up by the car which should have been at the depot before the bus started. When the news of the strike was told to the bus driver, he was equal to the occasion and explained to the passengers that we had struck but that the news had reached Northampton a bit late. The passengers were perfectly

United Counties strikers were hopping mad about working conditions under Tilling management in January 1936, as this illustration from Fred Marsh's book, *Busmen on Strike* suggests. (George Crutchley Jnr)

Another illustration from Fred Marsh's book shows a well-defended United Counties bus outside a factory. A small boy looks about to join in the popular support of stoning the double-decker, which already has a smashed window. A policeman is on hand to keep some order. (George Crutchley Jnr)

JUSTICE

for the

BUSMAN

" United Counties "
Profits

and the

Busmen's Case

United Counties' Employees'
Central Committee

1d.

Cover from United Counties union pamphlet. The document made an erudite case against Tilling's exploitation of bus crews. (George Crutchley Jnr)

good humoured about it and left the bus immediately. Although it meant a loss of time and money to them, they wished us luck and one old gentleman said, 'You damn fools, you should have done it twelve months ago!'

The bus crews were confident that public opinion would support them and that they would win.

By 8 January United Counties had sixty scab crews and twenty buses on the road. High unemployment further north made folk desperate and undermined workers solidarity. Labour was even brought in from Devon. The public boycott of buses helped the busmen and all vehicles were in before dark, which meant they were of limited use to local workers. Financial support form the public was crucial and strike committees organised collections. Buses were stoned and tempers flared.

Of Saturday 10 January 1936, busman Fred Marsh wrote that it:

> must be regarded as a red-letter day, for we had stood firmly shoulder to shoulder for a whole week and the feeling between the men was noticeably more comradely than it had ever been before. Our solidarity was favourably commented on by our fellow trade unionists…'

> A consignment of scabs from Darlington, the largest contingent of imported labour to arrive for several days, made its appearance during the morning and was noted to be dealt with later…

> The only systematic attacks on buses which took place were at Northampton, which had so far been a very quiet spot because the few vantage points were closely watched by the police. Now, however, a method of attack was evolved to meet the special requirements of the town. Its technique was unobtrusive and the requirements just one sharpened jack knife and a set of traffic lights. A position had to be taken up near the lights and, as the bus pulled up when the lights were against it, the knife was jabbed into the tyre when the wheel made its last half turn. Care needed to be taken that the knife was the right way round or the turn of the wheel would close the knife on the user's fingers. The trick was not very spectacular but it was effective and whoever was working it did considerable damage…

> On Sunday the public took a hand in affairs with a vengeance. They walked abroad intent on mischief and destruction.

> At Desborough the whole population seemed to gather in the High Street to do their damnedest to destroy any bus that ran along that route. Police reinforcements were rushed out and some buses were warned in time and returned to the depot. Others not so fortunate had a welcome which their scab crews would not easily forget.…

The violence, including trying to set a bus on fire, was getting out of hand. The strikers were informed that the Area Traffic Commissioner was threatening to revoke licences under section 74 of the Traffic Act. An inquiry was to be held at Northampton Town Hall on the following day. The inquiry was held under section 64 of the Traffic Act. United Counties were represented by their solicitor who argued that they had been unable to sustain services against such fierce union obstruction. George Dallas, JP, represented the unionists. The Commissioner implored both sides to settle their differences and get services back to normal. The busmen said they were prepared to go back to work under the old conditions, so long as all strikers were taken back without victimisation. The town hall gallery was packed with busmen and there was a deputation from the equally aggrieved London Busmen's rank and file movement who had given their brothers financial assistance. The same day a bus was hijacked and put out of action, even though it carried a policeman.

On Tuesday 14 January 1936, the traffic commissioner resumed his inquiry, saying he would take any necessary steps to get services running, urging both sides to give ground. United Counties agreed to reinstate all men, though strategies would have to be worked out to deal with seventy new men for whom there was insufficient work at that time. The busmen voted to return to work on the following day. Management agreed that in future men would not be paired with scabs. The commissioner refused to withdraw temporary licences granted to small operators who had been covering during the strike, until they were sure United Counties could be relied on to establish a full and efficient service. The busmen regarded themselves as victorious.

The way was now clear to continue rationalisation and modernisation. A range of new vehicles was purchased through the 1930s, in line with the company's anticipated and planned growth- in harmony with the rest of the expanding Tilling Empire.

With large-scale operations in mind, Bristol publicised their G, H and J range in 1931. Letters JW or LW were added to the type code according to which Bristol petrol engine was fitted, but the company was also experimenting with diesel engines, including the much favoured Gardner, which was denoted by an additional G. The last J type chassis was built in 1937, by which time all Bristols ran diesel units – there would be no need for the letter O in future model type designations. Re-bodied J types ran for years after production ceased.

There were no trendy marketing folk, in designer clothes, talking jargon and spinning yarns back in 1937. Serious fellows in dark suits or sports jackets, sucking pipes or twiddling moustaches, pondered the future of bus development because it was a serious business with no time to waste on flashy names, Bristol men simply superseded the J type with the K and L type chassis, double- and single-deckers respectively, revealing them at the first Earl's Court Commercial Motor Show, in 1937. By the late 1930s operators had a clear choice between high and low bridge types, with Bristol emerging as master of the latter type.

A 1931 AEC Regal, resplendent in cream/green coach livery. New to Allchin in 1931 the coach was purchased by UCOC in November 1933. Originally it was bodied by Duple with thirty-two seats, but re-bodied by Mumford in 1937. It was withdrawn in 1931. (R.H.G. Simpson)

Oxford depot's coach number 473 (Bristol JO5G registration VV6253, with a thirty-one-seat ECW body). It was used on the London Victoria service. Re-seated as a bus in 1952, it was withdrawn in 1954. On 1 May 1952, the Oxford depot of UCOC with eight coaches and the London–Oxford coach service was transferred to South Midland (part of Tilling's Thames Valley). At the same time 239 vehicles and the Midland operations of Eastern National were taken over by UCOC. (R.H.G. Simpson)

Tucked away at the rear yard of Oxford's Gloucester Green bus station, we see UCOC's Bristol 489. New in 1938, it was re-fitted to a thirty-five-seater bus, as seen here in 1952. We can see just enough of the Bedford OB to see that it carries wartime utility bodywork. A centre entrance Midland Red coach can be glimpsed on the far left. (R.H.G. Simpson)

A mud-splattered 472 Bristol JO5G ECW thirty-one-seater coach, new in 1937, stands in a muddy yard, with unsullied route boards, at the rear of Oxford's Gloucester Green bus station. It is waiting to be called to work the Victoria route. (R.H.G. Simpson)

The handsome lines of this Leyland TS8, HV Burlingham-bodied coach, are well displayed here. It was one of four, new in 1938 and number 508 in the fleet. All four were fitted with diesel engines and spent their lives working the London–Oxford route. The traditional Leyland vertical grille is covered with a sheet of aluminium for reasons unknown unless it was to help the engine run hotter – diesels run cooler than petrol. (R.H.G. Simpson)

A 1938 Eastern National Bristol K5G/ECW (641 in the fleet, registration GTW889), (*right*) makes a style contrast with a 1949 Guy Arab in Biggleswade Market Place. The Arab was new to OA Bartle & Son of Potton and passed to UCOC with thirteen others in 1953, when Bartle sold out. (R.H.G. Simpson)

This Bristol single-deck was new in 1938 and taken over by United Counties in 1952. Number 260 in the UCOC fleet, it had a thirty-one-seat ECW body. Eastern National origins are clear because there is no canopy over the half cab – canopies were favoured by UCOC. The bus was withdrawn in 1957. (R.H.G. Simpson)

Standing in a sunny sylvan setting at the rear of Market Harborough bus station, UCOC number 275 Bristol L5G with thirty-five seats, awaits the call to Lubenham Village, some 2 miles west. New in 1938, it was withdrawn in 1957. Market Harborough was Midland Red territory, but was served mainly by UCOC from the Corby and Kettering areas. (R.H.G. Simpson)

3

Pulling Together

The Second World War provided a common enemy and there was a more widespread attitude of pulling together – though this should not be sentimentalised or exaggerated. It was more a matter of urgency and survival than any other kind of enlightenment. Ron Blundell remembers:

> During World War Two the old single-decker Leylands were gutted of their seats and a row of slatted wooden seats installed on each side- so increasing the passenger space – no insurance limits then, it was a case of the more the better – with two rows of strap hangers. Also due to the black out regulations, the interior lighting was curtailed – the lights were dim and blue. A metal strip ran down the length of the bus along which slid a shaded light for the conductors who collected the fares.
>
> All in all, they gave a good service, especially during the war. They also delivered evening papers and parcels at appointed drops en route. The buses looked good in green and gold livery, with the minimum of advertising. Besides the official stops, the buses would also pick up passengers along the country road side; farm entrances, places like that. If there was a breakdown there was usually a long wait until someone realised the bus hadn't arrived and a relief would be sent out- there were no mobile phones.

The United Counties operating area was not greatly troubled by direct enemy action. There were some sporadic bombings, but the Northampton, Kettering and Wellingborough area was fairly safe. However, there was much to do for the war effort and 169 United Counties employees joined the services. The company also had its own Home Guard platoon. This grew into the 2001 Northants Home Guard M.T. Co., given the status of Command Troops under the direct command of DDS and T Eastern Command.

Petrol rationing reduced running from 8.5 million miles in 1939 to just under 7 million in 1944, while the passenger roll increased from 21 million to 32 million over the same period. Much of the running was due to the development of service camps, airfields in the countryside and factories for the war effort.

Many small operators thrived during the Second World War, when petrol rationing put a lot of cars off the road. New vehicles being in short supply, Bob Wesley of Wesley

Brothers, recalled working late to maintain vehicles during the war, ferrying workers to vital factories in Coventry and helping troop movements.

Wartime put pressure on resources and it was hard to keep up the necessary high standards of maintenance. Colin Wardle joined the company in March 1940, to train as a fitter, at the main works in Houghton Road. In his view the equipment was all of good quality, but there was no heating. Open fire braziers were used in winter. There was a brass token system for the issue of tools, each employee had five or six numbered tokens. The three inspection pits were side by side, with three rows of two benches in front of them. Entry was via a large door. After working there for six months, a young apprentice like Colin Wardle could get hands-on dirty work experience.

Engines in those days were lubricated by pretty basic mineral oil, which tended to sludge. Deposits collected in the engine crank case and parts were cleaned in a bath of trichlorethylene. The bath was about 10ft by 6ft by 4ft deep. With such fumes given off, such a system would not be permitted under current health and safety laws. Colin would soon be called to arms, but he learned well during his brief stint at United Counties, feeling that it set him up for a successful life in engineering, mainly abroad after army service. He said: 'In those days, I realised, for advancement you had to try to be a little bit better than the fellow on the next bench'.

Colin recalls that buses were docked for in frame overhaul at 30,000 miles. Then the oil pan would be dropped off, the cylinder head removed, with rods and pistons replaced where necessary. At 100,000 miles there was complete overhaul and refurbishment. At 7.30 a.m. the bus would be standing over the inspection pit, where a team would be ready to dismantle all mechanical components. The team comprised the engine mechanic, his apprentice, Bill Coles, engine fitter with his apprentice, Colin Wardle. In those days the front axle and steering system was handled by Harry Perkins. The transmission and rear axle was the responsibility of Albert Green and Bill Hoddle. Teddy Hayter and Stan Wood dealt with electrical aspects. Joe Abbot looked after radiators and the springs were repaired and made in the blacksmith's shop. If a bus came in on a Monday, it had to be returned to work by the weekend. After working the weekend, the bus was returned to Houghton Road for bodywork, covering accident damage and wear and tear. This aspect could take a week and the bus would be ready for the following weekend. In those days all painting was brushwork. There was no spraying. Mr 'Pop' Mayho was body shop foreman and Jack Craddock head painter. Colin Wardle recalled:

At that time people were jealous of their position in the hierarchy. My boss would say, he was showing me something but that I shouldn't show it to anybody else. You were made to feel very uncomfortable if you tried to rise above your station. Most people travelled to work by bus. My starting pay was 10 shillings and four pennies a week, with a free bus pass worth about 3 shillings and sixpence a week. From my pay, mother would take about 8 shillings each week, but I could buy a lot with what was left. Twenty cigarettes cost 1 shilling and a pint of beer nine old pennies. A bar of chocolate cost four pennies. There were five of us in the family. My brother George followed me to United Counties. The Chief engineer was Mr Gavin. His assistant was Mr Woods. Tom York was a long time employee in the stores. He worked wonders with just a stump for his left arm.

Fuel rationing also encouraged interesting alternatives, notably towing a gas-producing trailer behind some buses. Women were drafted in to help cover for men called up for war service, proving themselves more than equal to a traditional male role. UCOC had the ingenious idea of removing normal seating from their single-deckers, replacing it with bench seating around the perimeter to increase capacity to sixty plus standing room. In 1944 alone, the company carried an astonishing 32 million passengers.

The TBAT alliance lasted until 1942, with Tilling companies becoming identifiable by two distinct liveries of red or green, to match their standard Bristol ECW buses. Fifteen buses were converted to run on Producer-Gas, covering 417,000 miles and saving 61,000 gallons of petrol. Five vehicles were converted to bus ambulances and were operated by the Ministry of Health until 1944, while large numbers of vehicles were allocated for the evacuation of local hospitals should they ever be in danger from invasion or from serious bombing.

Most of the conducting staff were replaced by women and some of these became drivers. Evacuating the big cities was a major task and the company covered 27,000 miles, using 760 vehicles, carrying 38,000 passengers. Troop transport was another major task, carrying 28,000 men over 62,000 miles, using 914 vehicles.

Irene Mortimer was the first conductress in Aylesbury:

One had to be eighteen to get a licence in those days. The men conductors were called up so quickly. After a few weeks I was joined by three more ladies. The depot was in Buckingham Street, it was the Eastern National. It was a much better service. We shared the garage with United Counties. The company was operated by the same crews. Drivers Goss and Turney worked the route to Buckingham and Northampton, doing alternate shifts, one week early, one week late turns. Kingsbury Square was shared by Eastern National who covered most routes; Bedford, Luton, Amersham, Marsworth, Halton Camp to Tring station, Tring, Cheddington, Leighton Buzzard, Ivinghoe, and Slapton. United Counties and Oxford Bus Co. ran the Oxford–Bicester routes. Red Rose worked the route to Halton Camp, via Wendover. Osborn's Coaches ran to Halton Camp via Weston Turville. London Transport connected Aylesbury with Watford and Greenline Coaches started in Buckingham Street. Red Rover operated routes to Buckingham and Bicester and several villages across country. On all journeys, conductors carried ticket racks until new machines came into force. The earliest morning route was the early workman's at 5.30 a.m. from Southcourt. The last bus in from Bedford used to be 11.57 p.m. Most nights, during the war, there were two or three double-deckers full of airmen who used to sing all the way back to camp. Then there was the bus that took the displaced Polish refugees back to camp between Wing and Cublington. The funniest bus was the old 'standee', which held sixty passengers, thirty seated around the sides and thirty standing down the centre. The Luton route via Eddlesborough used to come back half-way from Luton, having taken passengers to Vauxhall and then on to Aylesbury. During the war the bus had a sliding light to conform

A wartime scene at Derngate bus station, Northampton – note the masked head and side lights. An attractive lady conductor, wearing a smart beige and green dust coat, adjusts the destination blind on 485. The bus is a Bristol L5G with a thirty-two-seat coach body and was new in 1938 – withdrawn in 1955 to become a driver tuition vehicle. (Gordon White collection)

A UCOC bus converted for
wartime ambulance duties.
(George Crutchley Jnr)

with the blackout and I carried a buttonhole light with a battery in my overcoat pocket. It
caused quite a problem in a crowd when there was an alert and only one light.

Meanwhile deep in the Northampton heart of UCOC land Ruth Eyres was serving the
wartime as a UCOC driver and conductress. She still thinks of the old days:

In 1941-45 I was a lady driver on the United Counties Buses. There were six of us doing
this dual job and my memories of conducting and driving in the blackout are still vivid.
During the blackout we had only one small light on each deck. Covered by a deep cocoa
tin shaped cover, which we pulled along with a piece of cord as we took the fares.

I remember watching the passengers stepping out of the very dimly lit bus, into the
pitch black country villages, to struggle home with tiny torches. On busy days we took our
turn driving double deckers out to Raunds, Daventry, Welford, Market Harborough and
Aylesbury. All buses had very small headlights, and though private cars were few and far
between, we often met long convoys of army lorries.

But I remember the cheerfulness of the passengers too, who in spite of long hours at
work and meagre rations, would joke and laugh with us. I remember seeing the excitement
of men in the forces, home on leave and boarding the bus home to see their wives and
sweethearts for a few short days, often seeing them again on their way back bidding tearful
goodbyes at the bus stop. On Wednesdays at Stowe IX churches one passenger who boarded
the bus to go to the cattle market at Northampton always presented the conductor with a
nice fresh egg. This was a luxury and carefully stored in our ticket box.

The inter-war years frightened the establishment into thinking that communism in
Britain, after the Russian model, was a real possibility. Party politics had collapsed and
Labour's first attempts at Government had been a timid failure. Arch Tory Winston
Churchill had been seen to save the nation at war and he expected his party to win
the 1945 election. The Tories, like all politicians, pandered to the lowest common
denominator, with all sorts of scare tactics, in their efforts to win the right to rebuild

This UCOC Leyland Lion is pictured on a hot summer's day during wartime. The windows are open to cool the passengers. Note headlight masks and white painted front wings to cope with the black out. Sixty years ago, passengers could be left waiting at the bus stand without risk of vandalism taking place. Number 164 in the fleet, the Lion had a Leyland body, was new in 1929 and lasted until 1952. The location is Oxford. (R.H.G. Simpson)

Britain, but it had been the people's war and they wanted the peoples party to represent them. The post-war Labour Government wanted the whole bus industry nationalised along with other vital infrastructure. With very good timing, a Labour Government was able to fit Tilling, almost tailor made, into its nationalising mould, via the Transport Act of 1947.

The British Transport Commission thus bought Tilling Group and hence the ability to build buses. Bristol were also employed to build lorries for the nationalised road haulage industry, British Road Services. Eastern Coach Works and Tilling were only allowed to supply Tilling and Scottish Bus

Everything was to be controlled by the British Transport Commission (BTC) through area boards covering the whole country. The standardised vehicles and liveries went unchanged, the BTC giving way to the Transport Holding Co. in 1962. BET companies remained private concerns, qualifying for a 50 per cent vehicle subsidy along with other private companies like Red Rover of Aylesbury. AEC became the major vehicle supplier for the non-Tilling companies, often with Park Royal bodies due to this supplier's continuing link with London General Omnibus' nationalised successor.

Bristol ECW buses had been restricted to nationalised operators until Leyland were allowed a 25 per cent holding in Bristol. In the long term this would see the eventually unwieldy and badly managed British Leyland Motor Corporation close down, before itself being nationalised, incredibly, by a Tory Government. Yet in the short term it widened demand for some Bristol products.

Returning to Northampton after the war, young soldier W.J. Hill saw a different nation, old hierarchies and ways of doing things much changed. During war service, en route to D-Day, his unit had been temporarily diverted to drive buses during the London busmen's strike – the strike related to danger money. The Hill's family business became main caterers for United Counties at Derngate. In those days there was still time to take care over such matters. He said: 'We supplied the basic foods they needed. United Counties had a very nice restaurant in Northampton. I remember the manageress, Mrs Holton. She was immaculate in her presentation. The kitchen was perfect and you could

Although from a damaged negative, this view is interesting as it shows the rear of the vehicle – most early views showed the front three quarters. It is RP6720, number 157 in the fleet, with a Leyland Lion chassis and Short Bros thirty-five-seat body. New in 1928, it lasted until 1952. The location is Oxford, the side of the ABC cinema presents the backdrop. That it is wartime is evident from the white painted mudguards and lower rear stripe. The Oxford City Council's adjacent fire engine, with high-level escape ladder, probably relates to the local war footing also. (R.H.G. Simpson)

New in March 1932, Leyland Titan (with Leyland body) number 257 in the fleet, is photographed during the Second World War – witness the white-edged front mudguards and masked headlights to make it stand out in the black out. NV1258 was withdrawn in 1951. (Authors' Collection)

The crew catch up with the news on Kingsbury Square, Aylesbury in this early post-war scene. The bus still carries white painted front mudguards and would have carried wartime servicemen to Halton Camp. The Dennis Lancet II bus with Willowbrook thirty-five-seat bus body was new to Queen's Park Coaches in 1942 and carries Bucks registration plates. It passed to Eastern National and then to UCOC in May 1952. By this time the company were standardising on Bristols and the bus was sold in 1953. (A.J. Reid)

have eaten off the floor. Father was an ardent mason. All coaching people were. We did a lot of contract supplying to caterers.'

War ended in 1945 and bus companies enjoyed the beginning of a boom after years of restrictions, with people liberating their desire to travel. Petrol was still rationed and railways were recovering from war damage, leaving buses and coaches the most ready to respond. Few vehicles were built during wartime. Bedford, a major local chassis supplier, had been busy on army work. Yet such was demand, any vehicle would do. It was impossible to get new buses and old ones had to be renovated.

By 1948, UCOC had joined the rest of Tilling in public ownership. Its east and south-east neighbour was Eastern National Omnibus Co., also ex-Tilling, operating mainly in Essex but running into Aylesbury through its Midland Division. Originally the British Transport Commission said it would not upset the Tilling Structure of operations and a Road Passenger Executive, chaired by George Cardwell, was established in June 1949, 'to review the passenger and road transport services operating in Britain with a view to determining the area with respect to which schemes should be prepared and submitted'.

The British Transport Commission wanted control of all bus and coach services, including private hire, except taxis. Fortunately the British Transport Commission got bogged down rebuilding and running the troublesome railways and Tilling Group Management had considerable freedom.

As already mentioned, UCOC, when they became part of the Tilling group, were constrained to favour Eastern Coachwork bodies on Bristol chassis. Bristol Tramways ran their first horse trams in 1875. Taking over the Bristol Cab Co. in 1887, they changed name to Bristol Carriage & Tramways Co. Ltd. Horse-buses were running in Bristol by this time, followed by electric trams in 1895. Observing developments elsewhere, Bristol experimented with Thornycroft and Fiat motor buses, making their own improvements and going on to build their own at Filton, north of Bristol. They were such innovators that they became involved in aircraft and high-performance car production.

Rule changes gradually permitted increased vehicle size, leading to longer and wider variants of the K and L types. Thus an LL was 1ft longer than an L and an LW was a widened L and a wide long variant was an LWL – width was increased by 6in to 8ft, beating the RTWs and Routemasters into new dimensions! The same codings applied to K types. If the vehicle was of the original shorter length an S was added to the suffix. Bristol aimed their double-deckers at the low bridge requirements. This was ideal to cope with a variety of industrial and rural limits. They achieved this through means of a sunken gangway on the near side upper deck, posing the problem of getting out of seats down below without head banging and cramming four passengers in a row upstairs.

The Bristol ECW UCOC tradition endured until Government legislation in 1947 forced Tilling to hand over its bus business to the Government. Eastern Coachworks went the same way, but at least they had a captive market in the nascent National Bus Co. – thus paving the way for the emergence of the Lodekka protoytpe in 1949. Nevertheless, there was a big shortage of raw materials after the war, and an urgent export drive to earn foreign currency. Britain was in debt to the US, big time, and struggling to disengage from empire. United Counties would have to make do with a lot of recycled Eastern National buses, transferred through Tilling's reorganisation.

By 1951, UCOC had carried nearly 41 million passengers, with vehicles covering 10 million miles. From 1951 onwards, the British bus industry struggled for funding and United Counties had the particular challenge of serving rural areas in an age of rising car ownership – Tillings as a whole suffered from this problem. Petrol rationing was on the wane and Ford promoted cheap motoring with their aptly named 'Popular' model and Morris offered the Minor, designed by Alec Isigonis. Isigonis capped his achievement at the end of the decade with his revolutionary Mini, taking more and more average earners off the buses.

With raw materials still in short supply and an export drive given priority, the bus shortage continued. The United Counties main works in Bedford Road, Northampton was thus kept busy putting new bodies on old buses Bill Horwood started with United Counties in 1952. At the time his father was working as a gardener for a wealthy family in Brampton. Rural England was still semi-feudal, in spite of Labour's best efforts – and the Tories were back in power. Because of his father's itinerant work, he had never been settled in school long enough to take the 11 plus and was told by his careers master that there was no call for his chosen work in carpentry, but that there was an opportunity for him washing bottles at the Corona soft drinks factory on Spinney Hill, Northampton.

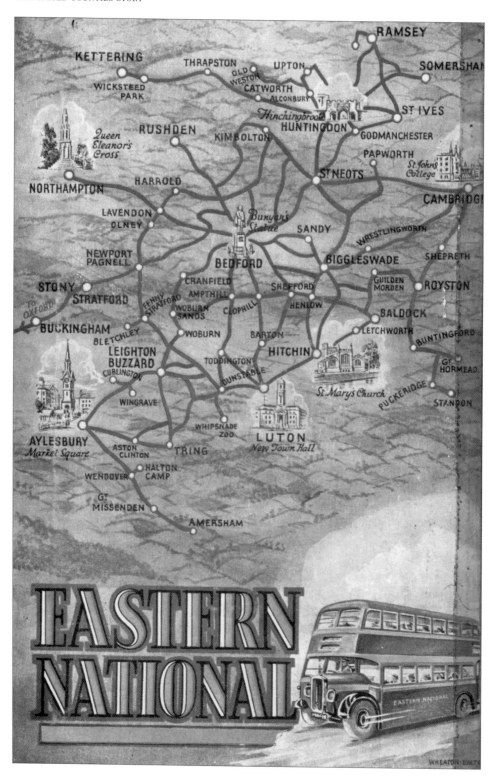

Eastern National Operational Area – western section, from the 1952 timetable. (Colin Harvey Taylor)

NOTICE

The Services in Bedfordshire, Huntingdonshire, Buckinghamshire, Cambridgeshire, and Hertfordshire which have been provided by **THE EASTERN NATIONAL OMNIBUS CO. LTD.**, are now operated by **UNITED COUNTIES OMNIBUS CO. LTD.**

Timetables for these Services are set out in the Midland Section Timetable Booklet commencing 16th March, 1952, issued by The Eastern National Omnibus Co. Ltd.

Full details of the Services included in the Booklet, or copies of the Booklet, referred to above can be obtained from the following Offices :—

			Telephone No.
AYLESBURY	22 Buckingham Street	...	Aylesbury 445
BEDFORD	Omnibus Station, Broadway, St. Peter's	...	Bedford 4161/2
BIGGLESWADE	28 Shortmead Street	...	Biggleswade 3175
HITCHIN	117 Bancroft and Fishponds Road	...	Hitchin 332
HUNTINGDON ...	Stukely Road	...	Huntingdon 159
LUTON	Park Square, Castle Street, and Williamson Street	...	Luton 5860

UNITED COUNTIES
— OMNIBUS COMPANY LIMITED —
HEAD OFFICE : HOUGHTON ROAD, NORTHAMPTON

Right: Notice showing intention to transfer western section of Eastern National to United Counties in March 1952. (Colin Harvey Taylor)

Below: A timetable extract showing the new service to Stoke Mandeville Hospital. Hospitals were thin on the ground in the 1950s and Milton Keynes didn't get one half big enough until 1977. The bus service from the outer reaches into Aylesbury were essential, hence the new service shown here. (Colin Harvey Taylor)

NEW SERVICE

STONY STRATFORD—FENNY STRATFORD—BLETCHLEY— LINSLADE—AYLESBURY—STOKE MANDEVILLE HOSPITAL

commencing SUNDAY, 1st FEBRUARY, 1953

LIGHT FIGURES DENOTE A.M. TIMES   DARK FIGURES DENOTE P.M. TIMES

386	STONY STRATFORD — FENNY STRATFORD — BLETCHLEY — LINSLADE — AYLESBURY — STOKE MANDEVILLE HOSPITAL	386

On the Fenny Stratford—Stoke Mandeville Hospital section of route, through fares to or from Aylesbury and Stoke Mandeville Hospital only are available

	WEDNESDAYS	SUNDAYS		WEDNESDAYS	SUNDAYS
Stony Stratford, Wolverton Road	1135		Stoke Mandeville Hospital	4 15	4 15
Wolverton, Opp. North Western Hotel	1140		Aylesbury, Kingsbury Square	4 25	4 25
New Bradwell, Bradwell Road	1145		Wingrave, Cross Roads	4 41	4 41
West View, Stanton Avenue	1148		Wing, Dove	4 48	4 48
Old Bradwell, Post Office	1150		Linslade, Cross	4 58	4 58
Loughton, Talbot	1158		Great Brickhill Turn	5 6	5 6
Fenny Stratford, Church	1210	1210	Stoke Hammond, Dolphin	5 10	5 10
Bletchley, Park Hotel	1215	1215	Water Eaton, Cross Roads	5 20	5 20
Water Eaton, Cross Roads	1219	1219	Bletchley, Park Hotel	5 24	5 24
Stoke Hammond, Dolphin	1229	1229	Fenny Stratford, Church	5 29	5 29
Great Brickhill Turn	1233	1233	Loughton, Talbot	5 41	
Linslade, Cross	1241	1241	Old Bradwell, Post Office	5 49	
Wing, Dove	1251	1251	West View, Stanton Avenue	5 51	
Wingrave, Cross Roads	1258	1258	New Bradwell, Bradwell Road	5 54	
Aylesbury, Kingsbury Square	1 14	1 14	Wolverton, North Western Hotel	5 59	
Stoke Mandeville Hospital	1 24	1 24	Stony Stratford, Wolverton Road	6 4	

PASSENGERS ARE CONVEYED SUBJECT TO THE REGULATIONS AND CONDITIONS OF CARRIAGE PRINTED IN THE COMPANY'S TIMETABLE BOOKLET

Head Office :   Houghton Road, Northampton   Phone 632   *Local Offices :*   22 Buckingham Street, Aylesbury   Phone 445
                                                                    Wolverton Road, Stony Stratford   „   3153

UNITED COUNTIES OMNIBUS CO., LTD.

See over

Cover detail from the March 1953 United Counties Omnibus Timetable. It shows the eastern and western operational areas of the company following Tilling's reorganisation. (Colin Harvey Taylor)

A rare picture of ONO999 when it was 4085 in the Eastern National Fleet before becoming UCOC'S 351. It is seen here in the snow at Main Point, RAF Halton Camp, on 3 January 1951, on hire to Red Rose Coaches – a sticker can be seen in the window beside the half cab. (A.J. Reed)

A fine portrait of 351 in Northampton Road, Kettering. It is a steep hill up to the town centre and the pitched roof of Kettering depot can be seen down the slope. The bus is an LL5G, new to Eastern National in 1952 and is on a Kettering town service. (R.H.G. Simpson)

Waiting in sunny Biggleswade is 822, another of the Eastern National KSW5G's, new in service in 1952 and then quickly passing to United Counties. UCOC served two busy RAF camps – Henlow in south Bedfordshire and Halton in mid-Bucks. With an empire to dismantle, national service was a duty for the nation's fit young men. Many a young man's last view of civilian life was getting off a green bus, before entering service life. (R.H.G. Simpson)

Apprentices at Northampton UCOC main works, early 1950s. Bill is seated at the front, almost centre. (Bill Horwood)

Kingsbury Square, Aylesbury and Bristol L5G KNO607, fleet number 308 is working the Halton RAF camp service. The bus was new to Eastern National on 1 May 1952. RAF Halton is situated on the scarp face of the Chiltern Hills. Behind 308 is a Lincoln green RT of London Transport and far right, we glimpse the back of a Thames Valley Bristol K. (R.H.G. Simpson)

The usual busy scene at Kingsbury, Aylesbury, as 711 loads for Halton Camp. This K5G was new to Eastern National in 1945, passing to Eastern National with the takeover in 1952. It has been re-bodied in this picture. (R.H.G. Simpson)

This L5G, number 333, was new to Eastern National in 1964. Here it waits on Biggleswade Market Square before working 5 miles north-east to Potton on the 190 route. The crew haven't bothered to change the ubiquitous 'United Counties' blind. (R.H.G. Simpson)

Bristol K5G, ECW. It was new to Eastern National in 1938, passing to UCOC in 1952, being withdrawn in 1957. Here it stands at Biggleswade before returning on route 176 to Bedford. Next to it stands a Biggleswade Urban District Council Austin A40 van. The pair of steps on the roof rack are marked 'Plumbers'. (R.H.G. Simpson)

Parked outside Biggleswade Market Square café is 320, new to Eastern National in 1947. Originally carrying coach seating for thirty-one, it passed to UCOC in 1952 and was re-seated in 1954 with thirty-five semi-luxury seats, for dual-purpose use. The basic destination blind shows only Bedford, ignoring the fact that there were two distinct routes. (R.H.G. Simpson)

An idyllic view of a small country market town, in the 1950s, as 591 leaves Biggleswade heading back west to Bedford. The vehicle is a Leyland PD1, new to Eastern National in 1952, passing to United Counties in 1952. UCOC sold it to Cumberland Motor Services in 1959. The windscreen on the ECW body slopes to accommodate the longer Leyland chassis. (R.H.G. Simpson)

Giving no indication of whatever this Aylesbury allocated coach is relieving, it is standing at Kingsbury Square. The bus was new to Eastern National in 1938, transferring to UCOC on 1 May 1952. It was withdrawn in 1956. The Bristol double-deck bus behind bears route 16 number, for Luton. London Transport's RT country service 359 to Little Missenden is just across the square. (R.H.G. Simpson)

A busy Kingsbury Square in Aylesbury as 818 waits to work the Raf Halton route. The driver rests his arm on the seat squab while the conductress peers demurely from behind the radiator grille. ONO79 was new to Eastern National in 1950, transferring to UCOC in 1952. Thames Valley's K is glimpsed far right, with its conductor exchanging a few words with a lady passenger. (R.H.G. Simpson)

Bill's dad suggested his son went down to United Counties Bedford Road headquarters, where he might be able to fulfil his carpentry ambition in the body building shop. Old buses were then being re-bodied and accident-damaged ones repaired. He realised that his father had decided not to go with him, approaching the large doors alone and with trepidation. Bill recalled:

It was a cavernous place. A man came up and asked: 'What do you want mate?' I asked if there were any jobs. He took me in and sat me down in an office and a chap came in. This chap asked me what sort of job I wanted. He was a squat sort of a chap and he said: 'I don't know if we have any jobs. We'll take you up the workshops.' It was a big place with buses stripped down, all the timber work exposed. There was a lot of banging and crashing going on. There I met Pop Mayoh, the body shop superintendent. He was an 'eh by gum' sort of northerner, a real stickler.

At the time he was busy making a great big shelf and didn't come to see me until twenty minutes later, in his office. He said: 'You want a job? You're lucky one of our apprentices has asked to change to the trim shop. If he gets the job we'll let you know. Then you'll come back with your dad to sign the papers.' Dad came back with me, signed the papers and I stayed on to work. Worse thing was starting at half past seven in the morning. As a schoolboy that time of day didn't exist! I had to go to technical school three nights a week and most of my day was taken up with work. The noise was the first thing that hit me, and I'd never seen buses in that sort of state. After two to three hours of being shown around, the noise sort of subsided.

To get to work on time, I had to run one and a half miles to the next village to catch the bus. By the time it got to Brampton it often had folk hanging on the back platform and would sail right by. That time of the morning you never saw an empty bus. Then I'd have to catch the next one at 7.40am. That was the office staff bus. They stared down their noses at the likes of me.

If a working man was a minute late clocking on, he'd lose fifteen minutes pay – a lot of money. The clocking on machines were just inside the wicket gate in the main works. The bus didn't stop near enough, so as it turned into Cheyne Walk, near the traffic lights – the lights were hardly ever against it – I jumped off the back platform. The camber was just right and you hit the ground running, running all the way to Bedford Road and the main doors. Many came to work on their bicycles. Drovers used to bring cattle up Cheyne Walk and there was a bit of spare ground leading to a sheer drop behind our works. I remember a cow got away, trying to escape its fate. It ran on to the spare ground and fell over the drop on to the bike shed. It did some damage, but wasn't hurt. They caught it and took it to the slaughterhouse.

Pop Mayoh sacked me twice, once when I was making rabbit hutches for him. He was God. Every hutch door had mortice and tenon joints. He came up to me and asked how I was getting on and was I all right. I said it was a bit boring, so he said if I was bored I could get out. I went to the union man and asked him what to do. He said to stay put, but if he Pop came back and chucked me out, then I was sacked. He sacked a lot of men. Some had come down from Coventry car factories. They had been working with hammers and screwdrivers and called themselves body makers. They couldn't do the job.

Tilling Management realised the world was changing fast and reorganised their operating areas. Accordingly, on 1 March, 1952, the Midland division of Eastern National was transferred to UCOC, an addition of 240 vehicles and premises in Aylesbury, Luton, Bedford, Buckinghamshire and Huntingdonshire. Other smaller gains included Aylesbury's Queen's Park Motors. Many small independent operators soldiered on, regardless of the large-scale co-ordinated nationalised opposition, patronised by a loyal following. E.M. Cain's Red Rover Omnibus Co. had gained a licence to operate the Aylesbury–Buckingham route in 1927 – previously operated by P.J. Simmons.

Cain was the son of a London horse-bus driver and the driving force behind the company. With his brothers he chose Aylesbury as the destination for an express coach route because he had an aunt living there. Roads were improving, especially after county councils took over highway maintenance in 1931, and pneumatic tyres made buses a worthy rival to railways. London's Greenline service came to Aylesbury in place of E.M. Cain's distinctive coaches. E.M. Cain's connections ensured that many ex-London Transport AEC buses would run alongside United Counties buses on the 46 route from Aylesbury to Buckingham.

The 1950s were still a busy time for coach trippers. Red Rover's Archie Cooper returned from years as a prisoner of war. Perhaps making up for lost time, as his friend and colleague John Payne recalled:

> Archie drove Keith Coaches excursions before the war. Then he was a POW. Afterwards he put on a lot of weight, so Keiths asked him to go on their Red Rover buses and Stuart Mills put me on the coaches. I learned to drive with Red Rover in Aylesbury. I was there when their first Bridgemaster (27WKX and number 7 in the fleet) came in 1962. It had been meant for Bartons and was a beautiful thing to drive.

Moving up to Aylesbury from London with his family, John Payne began his career on the buses with Eastern National in 1950, as a conductor. He left Eastern National and joined Red Rover after an argument about his right to take a day off to show his St Bernard at Crufts. He recalls Red Rover as rather a contrast to Eastern National, with characters like 'General' Clark, who liked a drink or more. Mr Keen, a coachbuilder, was standing in as the 'General's' conductor one night when the bus swerved round a double bend near Winslow, causing Mr Keen to fall off the platform while the bus was still moving.

When Red Rover was taken over by Keith Garages in 1956, John Payne transferred to drive coach excursions. He left in 1958 to become a conductor with UCOC, then back to Red Rover, where he got his driver's badge. He returned to UCOC as a driver between 1970–73. Among the characters at UCOC, John recalls Dot Fitton:

> She had two front teeth and a fag in her mouth – Senior Service. She didn't like giving change. If a bloke gave her a £1 note she'd take his name and address! One day she told a bloke to get off the bus, as it came through Aylesbury at Co-op Corner. He was a big bloke and he wouldn't move, so she hit him on the head with her ticket rack. She cut his head

Ready to work the 346 route, Aylesbury – Buckingham service, here is 934, a KSW6B, new to UCOC in 1953. A Red Rover timetable is visible on the wall, just ahead of the bus. Red Rover, a famous independent, was a competitor on this route. (R.H.G. Simpson)

Mid-1960s and Red Rover's first of two AEC Bridgemasters, rear entrance 27WKX. This was Red Rover's trunk route. By this time they were owned by Keith Garages, also a main BMC agent – Andrew Shouler bought a Wolseley car, decked out with polished walnut and leather, from Keiths.

'General' Clark's Red Rover overturned atop Oving Hill, on the Aylesbury Buckingahm route in 1948, in winter storms. Wartime munitions worker Gladys Close recalls having to get off the bus at the bottom of Oving Hill while the crew struggled to get the bus up it in the ice. (*Bucks Herald*)

Bedford Bus station, early 1960s and 791 stands alongside an early Bristol FLF. This bus was new to Eastern National in 1949, passing to UCOC in 1952. Bedford bus station was also fairly new, costing over £52,000 and taking eighteen months to build. It was opened by the Mayor of Bedford on 1 December 1960.

open and he got off without another word. It took about two hours to put all the tickets back in the rack. She liked her driver to carry her box. She worked on the buses during the war. She was a bit of a downer. I think she had been jilted at the altar. Still she loved her life on the buses. She could shift a bus load of people with a look. There was no messing about with her. Her regular driver was Rex Risley.

Another Eastern National Driver R.U. Palmer remembered Dot Fitten:

She wore an old brown hat and was the scourge of schoolchildren. I have seen her push them off with her ticket rack. She wouldn't let the passengers get the better of her and would never give change. At the end of the day her bag was so full, it pulled her to one side.

As a conductress she was supposed to change the destination blind, but she couldn't get up on the step. She would give the driver cigarette to do it for her, and sweets if he didn't smoke.

I started as a conductor on the buses when I wasn't long out of the army, in 1947 and I had been working awkward hours at the Co-op in Berhampstead. Mr Jolly was in charge at Eastern National. The manager was good, he always saw your point of view.

It was quite a job, a lot of figure work, everything had to balance. Schoolchildren could be awkward, especially the grammar school kids. They were supposed to have passes, and they would pass the same ones along under the seats. You couldn't let them get the better of you because you'd be in trouble if an inspector got on.

Inspectors had worked their way up from conductor or driver. They got better pay. Some were lenient, some strict and a bit officious. I never wanted to be one and be thought of in the way I thought of them. Two that I knew had been drivers and they changed.

With one of them you always knew when you were early because he'd swing his watch at you. When he got on he would check your tickets. I passed for driver in 1948. The test lasted 45 minutes and you didn't know the bus you were tested on. No two buses were the same. One of them, on a roundabout at Halton Camp, I had to put my foot on the side of the cab to lever the wheel round on the right hand lock. It was lovely on the left lock. That was 3070. Another bus had no speedometer, just a red light to tell you that you had were doing 30mph, and there was no automatic signalling, all hand signals. Some of the bells, ringing in the half cab were hellishly loud.

When we got the first new buses, with indicators, you still used your arm out of habit. When we got our first new bus, everyone wanted to use it. Then they put an 8 foot body on a 7 foot six chassis and I forgot the extra width in Kingsbury Square, scraping a car. Six inches made a lot of difference! I was driving one of the wider buses (KSWs) by the brewery in Walton Street and I took a load of washing out of a lady's hand because it was so narrow there. But driving was a pleasure then, with so little traffic and I was on my own up the front of the bus.

On United Counties as a driver, you knew when there was an inspector about because the driver of the bus coming towards you would flash his lights, because he'd just got off his bus and was waiting along the road. As a conductor you might let you friends pay fares for a shorter distance.

I liked meeting people. Some were awkward, but most were no trouble if you treated them right. Eastern National's garage was just a big shed, we had two mechanics and an electrician, but no canteen. When United Counties took over we got better buses. The new manager, Mr Jolly, was officious. You couldn't argue with him.

Tickets were stamped in denominations of pennies and shillings and the most expensive in my day was 4 shillings and sixpence and was a return to Bedford. On some Bedford runs, we changed crews at Woburn Sands, once a day. One time a tornado blew a tree down and we had to help passengers through the branches to change buses. That was my favourite route. Going to Bedford one day, we pulled up at Ampthill and there were two women fighting. They were kicking and pulling each others hair. I went upon the top deck to watch them.

There was plenty of time and a decent turnaround on the Bedford run. You only had time to do it once in day. You got a cup of tea in peace and could relax a bit. The worse run, I hated it, was through Dunstable to Luton. On the run from Dunstable to Luton there could be twenty seven stops and, as I said, some bells in the half cab were hellishly loud. The long run from Aylesbury to Northampton had its own dedicated crew and you only relived them on holidays or when they were sick.

John Payne recalled one very serious incident:

There were a few accidents. I remember as a conductor on Eastern National, we were going out to the displaced persons camp at Cublington, on a Bristol K double-decker. I was upstairs collecting fares and Little Willy, the interpreter, was downstairs. It was packed and one of these Polish blokes was sick over another. They pushed him to the back of they bus and kneed him off the platform into the road. As I came down the stairs, I saw it happen. When we got to the camp I reported it to the person in charge and he said not to worry, he'd be alright till the morning. When they found the fellow on the road, he was like a biscuit. They don't know how many had run over him!

We carried parcels and newspapers. One conductor, Harry Shouler, used to toss the papers off into the road. He didn't mind where they landed. It was just luck if they hit the pavement! On 1 January 1951, they put the fares up. I didn't know the old ones, let alone the new ones. Had to climb up the front of the bus and wind the destination blind to show Aylesbury for our return journey from Luton, that night. It was snowing hard and settling. Driver was brushing the snow off so I could see. Took ages. This bloke was watching me and he said 'Are yer goin' back to Aylesbury?' I said I hope so, I don't want to spend the night in Luton!

On the way back a furniture lorry hit us and I was shot off the platform and into the ditch. When I got my senses back and got on the bus, all the passengers had disappeared, except the bloke who had asked me where we were going. He said not to worry, give us yer hat. When I did, he filled it with money he'd collected from the passengers as they got off.

United Counties never made it easy for a crew to steal the company's money. Where there is a will there is a way of course, as Aylesbury-based conductor R.U. Palmer

Above: Tuition vehicle number 3 stands in central Luton before setting off into Luton's horrendous traffic, with the learner having to master a crash gear box (all gears having to be selected via neutral and double de-clutching), listening to the roar of its Gardener engine in his left ear and his instructor shouting into his right. New to Eastern National in 1938, the bus was withdrawn in 1956 to become a tuition vehicle along with its three sisters. (R.H.G. Simpson)

Right: An inspector awaits Bristol K, OND 79 en route to New Bradwell in the early 1960s. (John Royle)

recalled: 'All ticket machines were numbered and some of them could be used to the conductor's benefit. There was one where you wound the handle for the ticket and whipped it back quickly'. The ticket didn't register on the machine.

At company headquarters in Houghton Road, a team of ladies checked the Way Bills thoroughly. The total taken in fares was recorded on the back of the Way Bills. Conductors had to be good about their paperwork. Opening and closing numbers on ticket machines told how many had been sold. Parts of the ticket punched out by the conductor were collected and checked by the office staff. Small amounts were ignored, but pounds were not and there were ways of making a bit on the side, in a job that was not highly paid in relation to the stresses involved.

A big organisation like UCOC needed a lot of help behind the scenes, to monitor the cash flow, organise timetables and, with so much wear and tear to buses on the roads, the fitters were kept busy. Before the computer age, the paperwork from running such a complex business, including tons of lost property, was immense.

Mrs P. Croy worked in the traffic office at Bedford Road, Northampton, in the 1950s. She paints quite a picture of that bygone age:

On entering the office for the first time, it seemed like a huge 'classroom' with tables (not desks) set out like my schooldays. Everyone was friendly – and there must have been about two dozen of us. In fact around 16 of us regularly meet up for a Christmas meal. Occasionally, in between, and get quite nostalgic talking about the old times.

One of the things I was amused by, each morning happened when one of the girls took our order for elevensees. I was very partial to the canteen cook's scones – my batch of baking didn't 'rise' to the same perfection. On asking for the recipe, I was always fobbed off. Much later I found out why. Packets of sponge mixture were brought in and one just had to add the necessary liquid and mix in!

Another girl in the office was quite a skiver. She would go into the cloakroom and chat for ages. On returning she'd find a wag in the group had lifted her chair onto her table, but this didn't deter her from continuing with her escapades. Eventually she had a few weeks off due to illness!! She returned to collect her wages and no more did she return. We all understood she had been sacked – a common expression in those days. Her work was spread between two other girls and she wasn't missed.

I left for a job within walking distance of home but returned to UCOC when I had a small child and they allowed me to work from home. They provided a small adding machine and office equipment. The waybills which I used to process were given to willing girls to pass on to me on her way home by bus. I would wait at the bus stop at a certain time and my work load would be quickly handed to me before the bus continued on its journey. This carried on until I was made redundant owing to the fact that I did not belong to the union. As union members were facing redundancy, I was naturally one of the first to go. I enjoyed my time with UCOC and was sorry to see the offices knocked down to make way for more houses in Northampton.

Buses, like trams before them, were mainly for the workers as Walter Warwick recalls:

My memories of the United Counties go back a long way. In the early 1930s we didn't have a bus service in the village, but had to walk to and from Northampton to catch them. By the late 1930s we had two workers' buses at 7am and 8am, going into Northampton and later on, five o six buses into Northampton were introduced on Saturday. I don't know about the war years because I was away in the army.

I joined the United Counties as a conductor in 1959 and progressed to driver, in which capacity I served for 15 years. I recall one incident when I was a driver conductor. I was driving on a late shift one foggy Sunday night. In those days the only fog light was low down, trained on the near side curb. I was following the curb when I realised the road was too narrow as I could see the right hand curb as well. It was at the time when the M1 was being built and I had started to go down the slip road which had in fact been completed at junction 15. Luckily I realised I was wrong as the motorway at the time was not completed. I finally got my bearings and completed my journey, arriving back at the bus station about two hours late. After that night I was known as 'Foggy Warwick', name that stuck after I left – even today, if I meet ex-busmen. Luckily I never experienced fog as bad as that again on the buses.

I found working on the buses very varied and interesting. I particularly enjoyed the early shifts in the summer and of course the traffic was minimal in those days. I remember Saturday nights at 11pm in the bus station. That was the time for the last buses out. It left when the Inspector on duty blew his whistle. There would be one mad charge for the exit, but it was all executed with safety. We never had any collisions. I left the buses before the introduction of one-man operation as I did not fancy that at all.

John Pratt joined United Counties at Houghton Road, aged fifteen and a half in 1947, starting on 30s a week. He said it seemed a bit cheeky that Eastern National were then running a service that passed the UCOC's front doors. John explained:

I was employed in the schedules office, as a clerk, not an office boy. This was an important distinction. My department had to ensure that all timetables were covered by someone's duty roster. The situation was constantly changing due to factory and school holidays. We used big graphs to show the times of crews on duty. I was responsible for these graphs. We sub-divided the graph into hours. All was OK so long as we didn't make one driver late. If we did, we had to reschedule the next job.

We had similar graphs for tracking our buses. Northampton had about thirty double deckers and slightly fewer single deckers. We were constantly tweaking the system to get the best use out of our buses and crews. The attitudes were a bit more conscientious in those days. Reggie Howe was the traffic manager. He was a bit remote.

A big problem for a transport company like UCOC was the fact that there was a rush at the beginning and end of each day. Over a twelve hour duty period crews would do something like a 2.5 hour run in the morning, 1.5 hours mid-day and the 2 hours later in the day. For a turn of duty we would pay 8 hours 30 minutes and a spread over payment of 1 shilling and sixpence. If the period of work was over 10 hours and a driver had done 7 hours, you gave him 8 hours plus a shilling. At Northampton, drivers worked down the roster while conductors worked up it. This meant the same two people would work together once or twice in a roster. 'Drivers and conductors carried a working time table in their boxes, to comply with the Road Traffic Act.

We kept buses at out stations, like Silverstone, Desborough, Long Buckby and Thrapston because they had to be ready out there for the first runs into Northampton each morning. There were extra duties on Wednesday Market Day and for hospital visiting. Wilton Locks service only ran on Wednesdays. Early closing in Duston was on Wednesday so that people could take the bus in to the market.

There was a big build up of buses at 7.00am and 5.30pm, with maximum use of crews because that was the main means for people going to work. Kettering crews would be on the stand to relieve Northampton crews. British Timken in Duston had a big bus shelter. That's all gone now because the parent company can make roller bearings cheaper in Poland.

Reggie Howe was the transport manager during my time with UCOC. He was remote. Benny Goodman had a withered arm, but he was the artist and designed posters. There were a lot of girls on part of the first floor, with us. Engineering and accounts were upstairs, along with the canteen. Our food was prepared at Derngate and brought down in special containers. It was only two years after the war and food was still rationed, so getting a job with a works canteen was a bonus. Office staff ate separately from the manual workers.

Being near to Midsummer Meadow was handy for playing cricket in our lunch hour. There was also the open air swimming pool, near the power station. We had an office cricket team and played the corporation transport team.

I looked forward to National Service and when I returned life seemed different. I had mixed with other young men from different backgrounds, like shipyard workers. I was dissatisfied. I wanted £5 a week. I didn't stay long with United Counties when I came back from the army. I joined British Railways at Wolverton.

Like many who had returned from the wartime services, National Service widened men's horizons. Bill Horwood, however, was annoyed at being called up because he had just finished his apprenticeship and qualified for a man's wage. He resented National Service, being one of a group determined to do no more than the regulation two years. He said:

There was a lot of pressure from NCOs to stay on, but it always seemed to be the craftsmen and artistic types who wanted to get out. A lot of the people in the RAF with me were Scots and Irish where there wasn't a lot of work at home. Many of them stayed on.

The first thing anyone noticed about our works was the noise, but we got used to it and blanked it out. In the 1950s the office staff weren't allowed down into the workshop without permission and office women were not allowed down at all, except for Mrs Cherry, the bosses secretary. When drivers came to pick up a bus they had to go round to the front to get into the depot. We didn't see any office girls in our works until things relaxed in the early 1960s. Then at dinner time some of the girls would come down and sit in the buses with us and flirt. You didn't see people like the General Manager, Mr Pritchard. They never spoke to us. He lived in Olney and was chauffeured in.

Walter Warwick learned to drive the hard way, on tanks during the Second World War. He started at United Counties in 1957, but it was two years before they let him handle a bus. Missing the camaraderie of army life, the buses seemed a good substitute. 'I tried to get in a year earlier, but they weren't recruiting because of the Suez Crisis and fuel rationing. For two years I was a conductor'. Walter recalled his first day as a conductor: 'They sent me on the Raunds run. They did it to everyone. Folk were on and off the bus like flies, you didn't know where you were. Buses were governed then at 40mph'. On this point, another retired conductor/driver, Ray Fall, quotes Northampton's depot manager. Ray said: 'The manager, Mr Maycock, said whenever he saw a line of slow-moving traffic anywhere around Northampton, there was always a United Counties bus at the front of it. Mr Maycock was always a bit grumpy'. Walter is not a tall man and there used to be jokes with colleagues that his double-decker was seen entering Derngate with no driver.

Ray went on the buses in the early 1950s, having heard that there was a lot of money to be earned because you could do a lot of overtime. He said:

As soon as you started, the Union representative asked you to join them. Everything that went wrong you reported to them and they'd have a meeting, stopping the buses and leaving people stranded in the depot until it was resolved.

Shop Stewards just wanted things running properly. I remember the year I started they had a three day strike. We worked long hours for low pay. I started on £7.50 basic in 1953. Overtime brought it up to £17-18 if you did 100 hours – counting time and a half. There was also a half hour spread over payment. The long 346 run to Aylesbury was a good five hours. The company didn't bring out a pension until they had to in 1970.

Upstairs collecting fares was terrible, so much smoke. I decided to go driving. The conductor did all the work in those days. He had to know the fares and how to fill in a Way Bill, make sure the machine was registering and the money tallied. If it didn't the company took the deficit out of your wages. There were fiddles. If the bus was very full, the conductor might go very slowly and passengers put the money in his hand as they got off. There wasn't too much traffic. Motorists were considerate then. Of course it all changed, people stopped using the buses and the traffic got worse. I ended up with most of the work again.

Albert Houghton taught me to drive a bus. He drove it out to a road near the park, got out, I got in. He got in the half cab with me and sat on a little box, said put it in gear and drive off. I took my test in Northampton, passing first time, had to go all round town, reversing into the bus bays in Derngate. Mrs Nightingale was my first clippie. Ladies were as good as the men, though many had difficulty reaching the handles to wind the blinds. They got the same pay.

We used to drink. All the pubs were parcel agents. We delivered papers and carried mail bags chained to the back rail. It was unlocked at Derngate. Saturday nights at Derngate were very busy. We'd duplicate every bus out of there in the 1960s and the summer rotas were packed with excursions.

Inspectors would most probably be waiting for you in the villages. They'd pick the busiest bus and hope you hadn't got all the fares in. They'd check all the tickets and if you hadn't got all the fares they'd book you. We had a system where we could notify other buses along the way. The driver would flash his headlights at the oncoming bus so they knew an inspector had just got off his bus. As the other bus drove toward the waiting inspector, the driver flashed his cabin lights to warn the conductor. Who would rush around getting the fares in. The firm got round that by sending an inspector across country with a car and driver A good inspector was one who'd see your point of view and acted ordinary. I remember the two Cockerills, Wally and Sam were good. They were in their fifties and

Wally got a chest problem from being in Derngate for such long hours checking the buses in and out. There were a lot of fumes. Sometimes you couldn't see across the garage.

There were some accidents. I remember when they first built the dual carriageway from Roade to Northampton. The bus went into Northampton via Wooton. A lorry coming the other way flashed his lights at the bus and our driver assumed he was giving way for him to cut across. A lot of people were injured. Probably the best known accident was when Les Coleman caught the kerb with a double decker in May 1964. It took the steering and the bus ended up on the pavement wedged under a canopy. Les was a fitter and he'd only just collected the bus from Derngate to take it down to Houghton road works. One story was he swerved to avoid a cyclist. Bill Meredith was a conductor who always carried his camera and he nipped out of the Derngate to photograph it. They fetched the breakdown and parked alongside to stabilise it.

Driving a bus was a big responsibility. It weighed 7 tons empty and ten tons with a full load of passengers. It used to be affected by strong winds. Every bus was different, even if they were the same type. Some were heavy, some were nice and easy. I put it down to the tyres fitters cutting another tread in the worn tyres. They were designed for that, but you ended up with a flatter tyre which made the steering heavy. There was no power steering in those days.

Fogs used to be common then. One night I was out with little Reg Cox as my conductor. We got to the junction of Booth Lane and Wellingborough Road and stopped. Reg climbed on the mudguard to help guide me out. Another time I was just following the grass verge, all in the dark and the fog. The best view was on the 346 coming down Oving Hill, near Aylesbury. You could slip the clutch there and go quite fast. Going up you had to change down pretty quickly to get a good run at it. I used to buy sweets for our children, off the market, when I was in Aylesbury. I retired from driving in 1970 and went in the cashier's office.

Little Reg Cox was also remembered by Walter Warwick. Walter said:

A particular driver, Charlie, was famous for going the wrong way. Coxy was on with him this particular day. Drivers and conductors rotas worked in opposite directions, so they were not permanently paired. Coxy was a comic. He rang the bell and got off to check he had done the back destination blind correctly. He didn't have time to get back on and the bus turned left to Hazelbeech instead of right out of Derngate. When Coxy realised his bus had gone he went for the inspector and they sent someone out with the car. When Charlie got to Cheyne Walk and stopped for passengers, he wondered why no one had given him the bell!

The conductor was in charge of the bus, even if he did get less pay. Walter Warwick has clear memories of his early days on UCOC:

On my first day an old chap showed me how to use the ticket machine. Before you went out you had to know the timetable and how to use it. I had a couple of days with the old chap and them went out with a regular conductor, getting used to the fare stages and changing the machine as we went along. A good conductor was one who gave you the bell well in advance and a bad one was the opposite.

Some people could be difficult, most weren't. On the workers buses where we had those long bench seats upstairs, the fellow near the gangway would collect the fares for his row and hand them to me. Sometimes you'd get handed a two bob bit and the chap would say it was a half crown. You kept the two bobs in your hand before you gave the change. One late night run into Derngate, a chap got off with my conductor and I parked the bus. The chap attacked my conductor for his cash box.

There could be discontent if someone had more overtime or got long distance work. We had had one fellow, whatever the company suggested, he always objected. Bosses were very remote. When they introduced the 70 seater FLF double deckers, this particular union man said 'We're not having them because it will cut all the services. The bus company got its own back by sending us all the rubbish'. I also remember when a bus stop wasn't being used, he said we weren't going to stop there anymore.

In early pre-war years express coach services were still the elite arm of the enterprise, and driver Fred Newman's destiny. Fred left the forces in 1955, taking up lorry driving before joining Northampton Corporation as a driver. Here he met and married a young Irish clippie before going to work for Taylor's coaches as a driver. He joined United Counties in 1958. Recommended by Martin Kelly, he was soon on probation as an express coach driver. He found United Counties Express coaches delightful to drive after the demands of lorries and corporation buses. The Bristol RE was his particular favourite, in spite of the gear box. Fred was kept very busy with holiday trade. He said:

On Bank Holidays people went away for a fortnight, you'd have six coaches on a run to the coast, Bournemouth or Brighton. Express drivers had to be in tune with what passengers wanted, we needed a broad outlook. One of our coach drivers had been a pilot in World War Two and his face was all burned.

Race relations were not taken so seriously then. We would pick up Pakistanis in Birmingham and they would sit at the back of the coach. Inspectors at Victoria could be brusque with Asian passengers. Some Asians used to carry luggage in a special bag on their heads. They carried a lot of luggage and your boot didn't hold very much, nor your side containers. Some Inspectors were a pain.

The glory days were when you had the coaches lined up near Beckett's Park Promenade. In the Spring of 1967 we had a Mercedes integral coach on trial- registration OCH302E. Chap took us out on a trial run up the motorway. Air conditioning was new to us. In those days there was no speed limiter fitted to coaches, but we couldn't touch Midland Red for speed and the 70mph speed limit hadn't come in on motorways. Midland Red would come down the motorway at 80-90mph. That Mercedes coach would do 120mph. We had it for a fortnight before the clutch went. Mercedes flew a clutch into Sywell Aerodrome. It was so easy to change. I watched them. The whole engine swivelled out and the whole job only took a couple of hours.

The 1960s were going to be a time of change and white hot technological revolution. Certainly the bus design got better and Bristols brought out the Lodekka in the 1950s and it became Tilling's modern stalwart. Buses were also becoming technically more complicated, though easier to drive. Walter Warwick was en route to Peterborough, changing over with a bus coming the other way, at Thrapston, when he could not switch his lights on. Returning to the depot, he was a little embarrassed to be told that there was a master switch under the dashboard. The 1960s were still a little idyllic in places and Walter fondly remembers taking his bus through his home village of Collingtree, where his children and wife would watch him pass and wave to him. Though drivers' hours were unsocial, the family made sure they found time to do things together, even if it did mean taking picnics at unusual times.

The British bus industry, however, was set for decline on the service and manufacturing side. At least for a while, bus building was thriving and Britain was exporting them to Sweden. Bristol, Leyland and AEC dominated the industry and their progress was interesting. The Bristol Lodekkas may not be as famous as London's Routemaster, but they were the most ubiquitous type at one time, leading on to the best-looking adaptation of the double-decker to one-man operation, namely the VR. Bristol had moved more slowly toward the mid-engined concept than rival AEC, but in doing so they abandoned the conventional chassis for an under frame supporting running units to which a body was attached. LSX001 was the result and a basis for further advance.

The letter X denoted 'experimental', which meant that prototype Lodekkas would be designated LDX. Radical design allowed a central gangway on both decks and with no step up into the lower salon. They would eventually have a back platform door. Later ones had the luxury of Cave Brown Cave heating and ventilation. Eastern Coachwork attached bodies to a very low-slung chassis, permitting a very low centre gangway. With the engine still at the front, a rear-facing five-seater bench covered the transmission hump and the prop shaft split halfway down the saloon to two final drives. Tested around Bristol, further prototypes featured the familiar enclosed grille in keeping with the times. Over 1,000 were in service by 1958 and new regulations led to the 30ft-long LDL 70-seater. By 1959 Bristol had eliminated the need for a sunken gangway, allowing passengers to step easily in and out of seats. This modification was indicated by adding another letter F to the type description – for flat floor.

R.U. Palmer left the company for better pay in 1962, but got to drive the new buses for a short while beforehand. Some had the new automatic doors controlled from the driver's half cab. Passengers were as new to this novelty as he was, but there was no excuse for Aylesbury's UCOC garage boss's carelessness, as Mr Palmer explained:

I was driving the 6.00pm to Luton and Mr Jolly was on my bus going home. As soon as my conductor rang the bell, I pressed the button and closed the automatic doors, then pulled away. Next thing, I heard a lot of frantic bell ringing and looked in my mirror to see what was going on. Mr Jolly's head was poking out wedged between the two concertina doors which had met around his neck. I learned later that just as the bell rang, Mr Jolly had leant out of the door to say one last thing to the inspector!

Looking rather overwhelmed by Hitchin's mock Tudor shopping parade, Bristol KSG 788 passes a scruffy Ford 8 which is displaying its new-fangled direction indicators either side of the spare wheel. The bus was new to Eastern National in 1948, passing to UCOC in 1952. (R.H.G. Simpson)

Having left 575 at the kerbside, the crew are having an animated discussion. The driver makes his point firmly, but the conductress, with averted eyes, is not convinced. All this is taking place in Hitchin before the Leyland PD1 with ECW bodywork moves onto Templar Avenue in Baldock. New to Eastern National in 1947, it was withdrawn in 1956, having passed to UCOC in 1952. (R.H.G. Simpson)

Luton allocation 724 Bristol K5G working the 52 route between Luton and Baldock. New to Eastern National in 1947, the bus passed to UCOC in 1952 and was withdrawn in 1963. (R.H.G. Simpson)

This bus was new to Eastern National in 1950, transferring to UCOC in 1952. It went to UCOC in 1952, being withdrawn eleven years later. It is seen here in Sheep Street, Kettering on local service, 297. (R.H.G. Simpson)

Working a Bedford town service is 878, an ex-Eastern National KSW5G new to them in 1952 and passing to UCOC in May of that year. 'Carpet Sensations' are being advertised in the shop window, taking advantage of the 1960s affluent society. (R.H.G. Simpson)

The driver of 677 has his left hand supporting his chin, and is a picture of quiet contemplation amongst the hustle and bustle of a miserable looking and wet George Street, Luton. This bus was new to Eastern National in 1940, passing to UCOC in 1952, where it was re-bodied. Withdrawn in 1961, it was sold to Luton Corporation. (R.H.G. Simpson)

As we can see from the driver's hand signal, the bus is slowing down before turning from hilly Northampton road into Bowling Green Road, Kettering. Seen here on a town service, this thirty-nine-seat Bristol LL5G was new to Eastern National in 1950 and is on a town service. (R.H.G. Simpson)

This Leyland PD1 carries sixty-three-seat ECW bodywork and was new to Eastern National in 1947, passing to UCOC in May 1952, seen here around that time. The authors are bemused by the 7D route number displayed, as they can only recall the service as 131. Note its highly polished chrome radiator surround, in contrasts to the matt aluminium of the Bristols, and how ECW had to incline the windscreen to suit the longer bonnet. This bus is waiting at Oxford's Gloucester Green ready for the long run east to Bedford. The route was worked jointly with City of Oxford Motor Services, allowing the good people of North Bucks and Beds to glimpse an attractive maroon, cream and black liveried bus as an alternative to the omnipresent Tilling Green. (R.H.G. Simpson)

LIGHT FIGURES DENOTE A.M. TIMES   DARK FIGURES DENOTE P.M. TIMES

131   **BEDFORD — WOLVERTON — BUCKINGHAM — OXFORD**   **131**
Joint Service by United Counties Omnibus Co. Ltd. and City of Oxford Motor Services Ltd.

FOR ADDITIONAL TIMES BETWEEN : Bedford and Bromham, see Services 115, 128, 130, 132, 133 ; Bedford and Lavendon, see Service 127 ; Stony Stratford and New Bradwell, see Service 391 (Western Area Timetable)

No passenger may be taken up, at or between Stony Stratford, Wolverton and New Bradwell for the purpose of being set down at or between those places in either direction.

	WEEKDAYS				SUNDAYS				WEEKDAYS				SUNDAYS	
	UC	OXF	UC	OXF	UC	OXF			OXF	UC	OXF	UC	OXF	UC	
Bedford, Omnibus Station	7 20	11 15	2 30	5 55	2 30	6 30		Oxford, Gloucester Green	7 50	10 50	2 15	5 50	2 15	6 15	
Bedford, Midland Road Rly. Station	7 25	11 20	2 35	6 0	2 35	6 35		Gosford, King's Arms	8 5	11 5	2 30	6 5	2 30	6 30	
Bromham, The Swan	7 35	11 30	2 45	6 10	2 45	6 45		Wendlebury, Red Lion	8 20	11 20	2 45	6 20	2 45	6 45	
Turvey, Schools	C7 46	11 41	2 56	6 21	2 56	6 56		Bicester, Market Place	8 27	11 27	2 52	6 27	2 52	6 52	
Olney, The Bull	C8 8	11 53	3 8	6 33	3 8	7 8		Finmere Railway Station	B8 45	11 45	3 10	6 45	3 10	7 10	
Emberton, The Bell	8 11	11 56	3 11	6 36	3 11	7 11		Tingewick, Royal Oak	8 51	11 51	3 16	6 51	3 16	7 16	
Sherington, The Swan	8 16	12 1	3 16	6 41	3 16	7 16		Buckingham, Town Hall { arr.	9 0	12 0	3 25	7 0	3 25	7 25	
Newport Pagnell, Market Hill	8 21	12 6	3 21	6 46	3 21	7 21		{ dep.	9 5	12 5	3 30	7 5	3 30	7 30	
New Bradwell, Foresters Arms	C8 31	12 16	3 31	6 56	3 31	7 31		Leckhampstead Turn	9 11	12 11	3 36	7 11	3 36	7 36	
Wolverton, North Western Hotel	B8 36	12 21	3 36	7 1	3 36	7 36		Deanshanger, The Beehive	9 19	12 19	3 44	7 19	3 44	7 44	
Stony Stratford, Wolverton Road	8 41	12 26	3 41	7 6	3 41	7 41		Old Stratford, The Swan	9 24	12 24	3 49	7 24	3 49	7 49	
Old Stratford, The Swan	8 46	12 31	3 46	7 11	3 46	7 46		Stony Stratford, Wolverton Road	9 29	12 29	3 54	7 29	3 54	7 54	
Deanshanger, The Beehive	8 51	12 36	3 51	7 16	3 51	7 51		Wolverton, opp. N. Western Hotel	B9 34	12 34	3 59	7 34	3 59	7 59	
Leckhampstead Turn { arr.	8 59	12 44	3 59	7 24	3 59	7 59		New Bradwell, Foresters Arms	C9 39	12 39	4 4	7 39	4 4	8 4	
Buckingham, Town Hall { arr.	9 5	12 50	4 5	7 30	4 5	8 5		Newport Pagnell, Market Hill	9 44	12 44	4 14	7 49	4 14	8 14	
{ dep.	9 10	12 55	4 10	7 35	4 10	8 10		Sherington, The Swan	9 54	12 54	4 19	7 54	4 19	8 19	
Tingewick, Royal Oak	9 19	1 4	4 19	7 44	4 19	8 19		Emberton, The Bell	9 59	12 59	4 24	7 59	4 24	8 24	
Finmere, Railway Station	B9 25	1 10	4 25	7 50	4 25	8 25		Olney, The Bull	C10 2	1 2	4 27	8 2	4 27	8 27	
Bicester, Market Place	9 43	1 28	4 43	8 8	4 43	8 43		Turvey, Schools	C10 14	1 14	4 39	8 14	4 39	8 39	
Wendlebury, Red Lion	9 50	1 35	4 50	8 15	4 50	8 50		Bromham, The Swan	10 25	1 25	4 50	8 25	4 50	8 50	
Gosford, King's Arms	10 5	1 50	5 5	8 30	5 5	9 5		Bedford, Midland Road Rly. Station	10 35	1 35	5 0	8 35	5 0	9 0	
Oxford, Gloucester Green	10 20	2 5	5 20	8 45	5 20	9 20		Bedford, Omnibus Station	10 40	1 40	5 8	8 40	5 8	9 5	

*—Calls Lavendon (Cross) 7.51 a.m.   B—Buses stop adjacent to Railway Station.   C—Buses stop within 300 yards of Railway Station.   OXF—Operated by City of Oxford.
UC—Operated by United Counties.

INTERAVAILABILITY OF ROAD AND RAIL TICKETS exists on this route as between Oxford and Bicester, see page 27

TRAVEL BY ROAD AND SEE THE COUNTRY

The Oxford–Bedford service was originated by G.O. Gammond's Blue Coach Service in the 1930s. This timetable extract from March 1953 shows what a long haul it was for passengers and crew, even in the 1960s. (Colin Harvey Taylor)

Livery contrasts at Gloucester Green, Oxford. The City of Oxford Motor Services AEC Regent 863 stands ready for the 44 Witney run. Centre stage stands a shining KSW6B, about to work the Bedford 131 route. The bus, new in 1953, was still a youngster in this 1950s scene. They were such innocent times that it was possible for the side panel advert to bear the message 'Beans for the boys'. They'd never get away with that today. (R.H.G. Simpson)

Mr Jolly did laugh about it though! Working with people, I met some characters. One driver drove barefoot, you'd pass him and he'd have a great foot up on the dashboard.

One day this lady came puffing up to the platform complaining that it was too high for her old legs. I was there talking to my conductor. He said to her, 'hang on a minute, I'll lower the platform'. Then he wound the back destination blind handle a bit and she got up as good as gold, thanking him profusely.

Ray Fall spoke of a lady passenger bemused by the front entrance buses, with automatic doors. 'She walked all around my bus and up to my cab, then asked me how she could get inside!' Sadly it was not all fun and games and bus crew wages weren't keeping pace with the cost of living as the British economy struggled in the modern world. One-man buses would be a partial solution to manning problems, though it was twice the job for much less than twice the money. R.U. Palmer decided to leave. Ray Fall carried on until the 1970s but reckoned the one-man operation a poor deal. He argued that with a double-deck Bristol VR a driver could not be expected to take responsibility for what went on on the upper deck.

One member of the Northampton public expressed his annoyance with the quality of UCOC in Northampton. Writing to the *Northampton Chronicle & Echo*, T. Atkinson wrote:

The Waiting Game (an extract)

Oh it's nice to get up in the morning,
When the sun begins to shine
To wait at Buttocks Booth Corner
For a sight of the 329.
But the 329 is not running.
There's a shortage of a crew,
So we settle for the 302…
Our bus service should fall in line
And ensure that every morning,
We can rely on the 329.

Bus driver Walter Warwick responded with a poem of his own:

It's hard to get up in the morning,
When the snow is on the ground.
For I am just another bus driver
Who makes the wheels go round,
I may have finished the night before
At maybe ten or eleven
But I haven't had time to sleep or snore

I'm on again at seven.
Regular hours would be ideal,
A five day week just fine.
But what if I desert the wheel,
Who'll drive the 329?
My pay is low, my hours are long,
And I drive in rain or shine,
But I'm sorry to have done you wrong
Who waits for the 329.

For the time being there were plenty of characters to keep the bus wheels in motion. Walter 'Foggy' Warwick worked a lot of overtime to make up his pay in the 1960s, but he would not work his Sunday rest day. When he started in the 1950s he earned only £9 and increases only came in line with inflation.

Performance of the large companies suffered in the 1960s as wage bills soared. The United Counties area enjoyed fairly full employment and good staff were difficult to recruit and keep. Why sit in the half cab of a noisy double-decker at the beck and call of a bell nearly continuous in its ringing in your ear, with double de-clutching in the older vehicles, when you could be earning good money in so many different factories? From the late 1960s onwards, it was going to be something of a downhill run. Maybe it was time for some bold thinking about the future of transport, but they were the days of cash-strapped Labour wedded to the trade unions. The unions, for their part, mistrusted the bosses because that is what history taught them to do and it is why they existed in the first place. The rise of Margaret Thatcher and her reformed Tories would provide an interesting reaction to all the industrial strife that reached a peak in the 'winter of discontent' of 1978/79. When Thatcher came to power, the following summer, there was a hurricane of change.

Working on a Luton Town service and displaying an advert for a famous local product, Flowers Bitter, is 883, a KSW5G, new to Eastern National in 1952 – passing almost immediately to UCOC in May of that year. (R.H.G. Simpson)

Above: Working on the Luton–Baldock route 52, via Hitchin, is 771, a K5G, new to Eastern National in 1949, passing to UCOC in 1952. It was allocated to Luton depot. (R.H.G. Simpson)

Opposite below: Heading for Derngate prior to entering the bus station, heading from Daventry on service 311, is this Bristol, JO5G fleet number 211. It was new in 1938 and re-bodied and given a 'low' PV2 radiator in 1951. It was withdrawn in 1960. (R.H.G. Simpson)

Ex-Eastern National Bristol resting in Biggleswade in the early 1950s. Note its Essex registration GTW889. New in November 1938, it passed to UCOC on 1 May 1952. It was at least fifteen years old when photographed and bears its age well. (R.H.G. Simpson)

Another of the 220 vehicles transferred from Eastern National when United Counties took over their Midland area services on 1 May 1952. New in 1940, Bristol K5G JEV412 was re-bodied in May 1953, surviving in the UCOC fleet until September 1960. It was then transferred to the hilly terrain of South Wales's United Welsh – quite a change from the flatlands of east Bedfordshire. It is photographed in Biggleswade. Far right we can see one of the attractive signs put up throughout Bedfordshire to commemorate the Festival of Britain in 1951. (R.H.G. Simpson)

Left: Veteran driver and TGWU shop steward George Crutchley with a 1938 Bristol JO5 G at Northampton depot in the late 1950s. George was a strong union man, holding meetings at home in his front room. (George Crutchley Jnr)

Below: This KSW6B may have been new in 1952, but its style was starting to look dated here in mid-1950s Northampton, as it approaches Derngate from West Haddon, along the Rugby Road, 15 miles away. (R.H.G. Simpson)

Bus design developed rapidly through the late 1940s and '50s. This smart Bristol L6B with ECW thirty-one-seat bodywork was new in 1948 and transferred to South Midland in May 1952. It is waiting here at Gloucester Green, Oxford, to work to Victoria. A new generation of coaches were gradually replacing this majestic style, with origins going back to the 1930s. (R.H.G. Simpson)

Gloucester Green again and a fine old Wolseley car has its nose up against the chain link fence. New in 1951, this LL6B Bristol (836 in the fleet) stands ready for the London run. Fitted with an ECW 37 coach seat body, at the time of this photograph it had already passed to South Midland in 1952 as no. 78 (number just above the headlights), when they took over UCOC's Oxford operations. (R.H.G. Simpson)

New in 1957, fleet number 115 waits on the seafront at Brighton. The LS6G chassis carries a later version of the ECW coach body. The addition of front roof lights meant destination boards had to be repositioned under the windscreen. Curved windscreen quarter lights have made way for wider screens. This coach was sold to Eastern National in March 1962, becoming their 024. (R.H.G. Simpson)

The driver's smart green and cream summer dust coat catches the sunlight as this Bristol LL6B accelerates away from Victoria, 833 is about to head north for Northampton, Leicester and Nottingham. The modern full-fronted ECW thirty-seven-coach seat body contrasts with the elderly London London Austin cab. (R.H.G. Simpson)

4

HAPPY DAYS

When buses were new to UCOC, the fleet number colour coding was rigidly adopted, but later when the 'elderly vehicles' were shuffled between garages the colour coding was often not changed. Northampton had the Lion's share of new vehicles because it was the premier depot, working the premier Northampton, Leicester, Northampton and London express routes along with the Associated Motorways pool. The year 1966 is particularly significant when looking at the state and size of the fleet.

In 1966 fleet strength was 476 allocated as follows:
Aylesbury, Buckingham Road (fleet number badge blue background and red stripe) 21 buses.
Bedford, St Johns (fleet number badge blue) 70 buses.
Biggleswade, Shortmead Street, (fleet number badge blue and black) 91 buses.
Corby, Station Road (fleet number badge yellow and black) 14 buses.
Hitchin, Fishpond Road, (fleet number badge brown and black) 18 buses.
Huntingdon, Stukeley Road, (fleet number badge blue and yellow) 12 buses.
Kettering, Northampton Road, (fleet number badge yellow) 12 buses.
Luton, Castle Street, (fleet number badge brown) 69 buses.
Northampton, Houghton Road, (fleet number badge green) 95 buses.
Rushden, Newton Road, (fleet number badge red and black) 17 buses
Stony Stratford, Wolverton Road (fleet number badge green and black) 16 buses.
Wellingborough, St Johns street, (fleet number badge red) 27 buses.
The above total adds up to 423 with the shortfall of 53 accounted for by overhaul, accident damage and depot float.

The year 1966 was significant because it was only a year before release of expansion plans for Northampton and for the neighbouring development of a large rural area into the giant new town of Milton Keynes. At that time Corby still had its steel works and Luton still ran reasonable works services to Vauxhall, Skefco and Electrolux, so it was indicative of the state of the company just before the dawn of the National Bus Co. and the moribund onset of the 1970s and industrial strife. The fleet was expanded a little

Carrying factory workers was a major part of UCOC's business. This is Kimpton Road, Luton and shift change at Vauxhall Motors in the 1950s. Buses also came from as far away as Aylesbury to serve the AC Delco factory in neighbouring Dunstable. (Vauxhall Motor Co.)

in 1970 when UCOC took over Luton Corporation's operation. In 1975 UCOC also expanded routes, taking on all York Brothers stage routes, but none of their vehicles.

Companies like Red Rover had a core of reliable stalwarts throughout the 1960s, undoubtedly with a soul above money. Like the fleet, they were a motley crew, characters all, to match their vehicles. Cain sold out to Keith Garages, becoming part of their Keith Coaches Bicester Road operation in 1955. Before the war, car ownership had been the province of the better-off and something for the lower-middle classes to aspire to. By 1940, car ownership had reached 2 million. Prime Minister Harold Macmillan informed the nation in 1959 that they had never had it so good – hire purchase fuelling the boom.

Cars were changing the national landscape. Ownership doubled from 5.6 million to 11.8 million during the 1960s. By the end of the decade, 600 miles of motorway had been completed and the railways were being decimated. This was not a good time for public transport. Few people saw the dangerous trend that would prove impossible to halt because money was being made.

In April 1964 the *Bucks Herald* reported that a UCOC proposal for an express coach link from Stevenage to Oxford through Aylesbury had been turned down. Alderman

One of Luton Corporation transport's Dennis Lolines with East Lancs bodywork, new in October 1960 – it had appeared on the Dennis stand at the 1960 Commercial Motor Show. Here in Luton Corporation's red and cream. It would be repainted into UCOC's green and cream, and re-numbered 824 following the takeover of January 1973. The bus was withdrawn in July 1973. It was one of seventy-seven vehicles, both single- and double-deck, acquired by UCOC. The state of these buses placed considerable strain on staff at UCOC main works. (R.H.G. Simpson)

In recent years Steeple Claydon-based Langston & Tasker have done contracting over part of the old UCOC 121 route from Winslow to Bletchley. Here one of the firm's founders, the late George Tasker, drives his bus to the seaside, through the increasing traffic congestion consequent to increasing car ownership in the late 1950s. (Maurice Tasker)

Some attempts have been made to co-ordinate bus and rail services, but not perhaps with old-fashioned thoroughness. This is 982, a Northampton-allocated LD6B Lodekka. New in 1955 it was one of a batch of twenty-eight, numbered 971–955, supplied from 1955–6. This bus is parked alongside the Bedford–Cambridge railway line at St John's depot. The A6 London Road crosses the railway behind it. (R.H.G. Simpson)

W.A. Narbeth called the Licensing Authority 'these little self-appointed dictators' and warned that people would soon be 'in a slave state'. Councillor L.J. Bourke called it a blow for Aylesbury, arguing that the proposal would significantly shorten the journey time between Aylesbury and Oxford. There was little in the way of vision for the development of public transport. The motorway boom would ultimately benefit the coach industry as it adapted itself to new markets. The initiative came from a Tory Transport Minister, Ernest Marples, who was involved with road constructor Marples Ridgeway.

Marples' enthusiasm to destroy the railways was understandable and he employed a friend, chemist Dr Richard Beeching, to help him do it. Beeching did not, however, agree to close the rail route that cut right through UCOC territory from west to east – namely the Oxford to Cambridge line. That decision was made by Labour Minister Barbara Castle, a lady much admired by Tory Michael Heseltine in his memoirs, for her attitude to public transport.

Barbara Castle's decision to close the Oxford–Cambridge railway line in 1967 came at the dawn of Milton Keynes' heyday and makes no strategic sense. True, the railways had suffered from restrictive practices that no party had tamed and the country was nearly bankrupt. However, the Buckingham MP Robert Maxwell commented: 'I have been convinced all along that the Ministry of Transport and British Railways have made a ghastly mistake... Bus operators can only provide a service on this line at the expense

Twin Bristol MWs rest at Victoria Coach Station after traversing two different routes to reach the London metropolis. Number 150 had come via the country route of Woburn, Dunstable, Luton and St Albans. Number 159, on the right, had hurried down the motorway express route. That was all in half a day's work for these stalwarts of the early 1960s. (R.H.G. Simpson)

of providing an even worse service...on other routes in the area'. This was a period of great difficulty recruiting bus crews. Shift work, declining real pay and more awkward customers in the youth-orientated 'Swinging Sixties' offered little encouragement.

Those were also the years of Wilson's Labour Government and, like today, a massive balance of payments deficit. Trade unions held the Government to ransom, inflation was off the scale and strikes handicapped the economy.

One solution to labour shortage was to employ part-timers but this was a threat to wages as far as full-timers were concerned. John Royle, now living in Canada, recalls working part-time for UCOC during 1965–67. He said:

At that period I was living in Deenshanger but only worked out of Derngate and that was just on Saturday, pm. As a part-timer we were restricted as to our routes owing to not all the garages were in the agreement with the union on the situation, so the company made certain that we didn't stray into militant territory. Stony Stratford was particularly bolshy and there was one occasion when I worked in on the 326, I think, with a regular conductor. I made myself scarce on arrival but the conductor had some fancy talking to do at departure time, so did I. However, as I was in full uniform, I pulled it off – many of the part-timers had only a dust jacket to wear. Still on arrival back at Derngate I was told not to make the same mistake again. Our work was mainly on 305, 306, 307, 308, 309, 311, 312, 322, 323, 329, 345 and with a few trips to Kettering or Wellingborough if someone suddenly went sick.

Here we see number 312 on the 121 service from Oxford to Bletchley, via Bicester and Winslow. It was a latter-day replacement for the defunct Oxbridge line and was operated jointly with City of Oxford Motor Services. It petered out in the early 1980s, having been very unreliable in the authors' experience. MK Metro and Langston & Tasker are among several who have since offered limited service on parts of the route. (R.H.G. Simpson)

Pristine newness is apparent as TRP560 exits Eastern Coach Works in Lowestoft. Its aluminium fleet number plate 560 is still to be fitted, as are the UCOC destination and number blinds. The bus is an LD6B with a fifty-seven-seater body, complete with state-of-the-art platform doors. An Eastern National MW with open windscreen is in the background. (R.H.G. Simpson)

Dave O'Dell was another part-timer at Northampton in the 1960s. He said he always wanted to work on the buses but the pay did not compare with factories or the engineering work he was doing at the Express Lift Co. He said:

> I approached them for driving duties but worked firstly as a conductor because the company would not pay for my training as a part-timer. I started as a conductor in 1962, often working with John Royle. I suppose it was in my blood. My dad drove a bus for Yorks. We weren't flavour of the month with the unions, though they allowed it if we were in another union. I was in the AEU. Some of them had an attitude to us, but they didn't want to do the late duties and didn't want anyone else to do them. Some of the branch union officers rubbed it in a bit. We might get called in to do the late 8.30pm run to Corby, possibly paired with one of the regulars. If I was conducting I liked to be on a Lodekka with doors and a heater. Those old K types with the open platform were cold in the winter.
>
> Folks weren't too bad then, though some young ones played up a bit. There used to be two buses leaving at 11.00pm, going along the Weedon Road. One went to Daventry, the other to Upper Weedon. I was on the second bus, following the other one and saw some yobs pulling out the upper deck lamps and throwing them out of the windows. The following Saturday I had a police sergeant at Derngate to back me up when I wouldn't let them on the bus. They tried to cut across town and get on the other one, but they didn't succeed. We never saw them again.
>
> There was a need for extra drivers to cover services during the summer, while full-timers did the excursion work, and they used to advertise. In 1964-5 they decided they could afford to train part-timers to drive and I applied. Part-time work ended around 1971 because they didn't have enough buses on the road by then.

Stony Stratford was also known for its conflicts with workers from nearby Bletchley Garage, there being a predominance of rural characters at the former and cockney newcomers at the latter. Multi-culture was not the thing then that it is today and tribalism had a free rein. Trade unionism was very strong in the 1960s and management was often high-handed. It was an 'us and them' situation which came to a head when Margaret Thatcher became Prime Minister. John Royle explained:

> I was born and brought up in Manchester and after demob in 1946, my father went onto the buses with Manchester Corporation, my treat was to ride for free on mainly Daimlers from Sharston Garage.
>
> Part-timers working for United Counties had to be in a union otherwise the T&GW wouldn't allow you. At the time I was in the print as a compositor. Originally I was on the back as a conductor, but was putting myself through the PSV test privately at a school in Nottingham, but UCOC got to hear about it and offered to put me through the test in Northampton. It was all very hush hush so as not to upset the local committee. The man who became my conductor, Dave O'Dell, was an electrical engineer and we remain good friends to this day.

The trade union's attitude was understandable. As George Crutchley explained:

> There were many TGWU meetings at my house. My father worked through the harsh war years. He was very left wing, very political, but that was only because he wanted better conditions for his men. One of his timetables shows him doing an 80 hour week. I don't know whether he actually did that.

Working hours were not so strictly regulated until the end of the 1960s when European standards started to take effect. Using part-timers to plug the gap was of only limited use. Trade unionists resisted not only an influx of part-timers, but women also. One benefit of using part-timers was that they were often great bus enthusiasts. John Royle said:

> I was interested in buses from when my father was demobbed from the army in 1947 and went to work for the MCTD at Sharston Garage, at Northenden in Manchester. I was working as compositor in the printing trade and living at Deanshanger when I applied for part-time work on UCOC. I was taking lessons in Nottingham and trained on a Leyland PD2. It had a wicked gearbox and most of my time was spent trying to master it. When UCOC found out what I was doing they invited me for trial on their trainer, ex ENOC K type, registration ONO 73. It was a dream. I never missed a gear and the company offered to put me through the test there and then and I passed first time. None of this was divulged to the TGWU or regular staff on the UCOC.
>
> Not everyone was hostile. It was only Northampton Garage that would allow part-timers and of course the duties were only ones that the men wanted to get out of on a Saturday afternoon/ evening. Many of them were pleased to get the day off and there did not seem to be many who wanted the overtime. It was not often that us part-timer got offered overtime and if we were, it would be before the regular duty time.
>
> It would be difficult for the company to roster us before the start of duty and it would be a part-timer's responsibility to telephone in and enquire if needed. However, some garages like Stony Stratford and Bletchley, would not even entertain a part-timer coming into the yard, so Northampton made sure you never did. As long as you belonged to a Trade Union affiliated to the TUC you were not required to join the TGWU. However, the TGWU did check you out to see whether you were legitimate. My print union were not impressed and thought I was acting beneath myself by wanting to go on the buses, In those days the print unions were top dogs when it came to crafts.
>
> Pay then was almost less than half what I was making at the trade, however, it was more for the work experience and not the money that I did it, really, I would have gone in for nothing as long as I was around buses. As part-timers we generally started around 1400 hours, it could have been slightly earlier and the shifts ran to around midnight or slightly later. The work offered was only on Saturdays.
>
> The worst routes were those that went east towards Wellingborough and Corby, mostly because the passengers were more likely to be difficult, especially in Corby, these routes were not generally offered to PTs but not unknown either. I always enjoyed the Daventry road for country and in town the 321 group to Duston, only a short route but busy enough

Number 560 from the previous picture has covered some miles since that picture was taken. Here the Lodekka trundles through Brixworth in the early 1960s. (John Royle)

Number 560 parked up in Brixworth, the conductor adjusts the destination blind ready for return to Northampton. (John Royle)

A Bristol K, number 933, exiting Derngate in the early 1960s. The site is now a theatre complex. (John Royle)

to give you an interest and there was always the Northampton Corporation buses to race! The buses used on the route were generally the K types, known by the drivers as sewing machines, lovely little buses to drive and work with on such a route.

Derngate was the typical Tilling bus station, well placed for the town centre and was never a problem on entering, leaving or finding a parking space for your bus. The canteen was good and well run. According to John's memory it was:

Part-time driver John Royle with his bus at Brixworth in the early 1960s. (John Royle)

a lively place late on Saturday nights with rowdy passengers, the last buses back to the villages all left at 2300 and the buses were backed onto the stand and left to fill up, fights used to break out even before departure and the town police usually were in attendance whether called or not. One incident I recall was in connection with an Irish police sergeant who was feared by the yobs. A fight had broken out on the top deck of the bus and on hearing the police arrive, down the stairs they came. To escape, one lad rolled under the bus and refused to come out. The sergeant ordered me to start the engine. He still stayed underneath. The sergeant then asked for me to put it in gear and drive away. Selecting a gear to make a lot of noise about it was enough for the lad and out he came into the arms of the law. Mostly though names were taken and they were allowed back on board, any problem on the journey and of course the conductor knew who to report.

I daresay the sergeant's actions would be frowned on today but in those days it was just the way things were done and no-one really was concerned, although the yobs could be a rowdy bunch, it was only fists, boots and yelling, not the mindless violence of today, they also respected uniforms a lot more as well.

A bus driver's pay was less than half of what John was making at the trade. However, as he said, he would have done the job for nothing, so long as he was around buses. As part-timers they generally started around 1400 hours, it could have been slightly earlier and the shifts ran to around midnight or slightly later.

Even though part of a large group, UCOC seemed to think of itself as a 'local concern', the good old ways have certainly vanished from the scene in these days of the make an obscene profit at all costs mentality. John Royle said:

A rain-washed 357 drives back to its base, the White House at Stony Stratford. It has been out on the twice-weekly market day service to Aylesbury via Winslow. This service was favoured by Winslow folk as a faster alternative to the 346 which travelled all around the villages. UCOC bought the grand White House, building a garage in 1953. FRP822 was new in 1950 and withdrawn in the late 1960s, along with this service. (R.H.G. Simpson)

Standing outside Stony Stratford garage is 721, a Bristol K5G with ECW fifty-five-seater bodywork. New in 1947, it was withdrawn in 1963. The blind is misleading, 3276 ran from Wolverton to Buckingham. (R.H.G. Simpson)

The worst I ever had to experience was being shown a knife when requesting a fare, this was on a last bus out to a village, we didn't go round to get the fares in until we passed the boundary stop on leaving Northampton, so by the time of my incident we were out in the country. This passenger had done this on a previous weekend and the inspector told me not to press for the fare but report any problem as the company was building a case against the youth to have him banned from riding.

I had not noticed but a passenger from downstairs had followed me up, pushed me in the back and leaned into the seat and punched the lad in the face, dragged him down the stairs and I followed them down. The big fella was saying he had had enough of this sort of disruption every week and he, his wife and all the other villagers were tired of it, the lad was going to have to walk home. I went to ring the bell for an emergency stop but the man just pulled open the doors (back loader) and out went the youth with us bowling along at around 30mph.

The sound of screams and crashing through a hedge came from outside and his mates came down and demanded to go to his aid, I stopped the bus, the driver had no clue as to what had happened, but with the lads off, the passengers suggested we move on.

Next week, I was on the same trip again, our knife carrier was on board, face heavily scratched and an arm in plaster, he handed over his fare without a word and the big man and his missus were sat downstairs and never mentioned the previous week. As I said things were settled different then and to my mind much better. The UCOC were aware of the incident and just let it go with nothing said.

From John Royle's viewpoint many of the younger conductors seemed to think females were all looking for a good time with them. As for the clippies everyone got on well together. The clippies at Northampton mostly seemed to be only interested in doing the job and earning a wage, John said:

I only recall at Northampton two who stood out as trying to attract the blokes, they were actually mates but used to see how far they could go with making the uniform as attractive as possible, it was all very good natured stuff.

I recall at one point there was a certain Irish conductor, he was married, was taking out one of the clippies as well as one of the regular lady passengers, all three women were not aware of each other or of the fact that they were all pregnant by him, he suddenly left during his duty, taking the passenger off to Ireland to avoid the law.

John said conductors had to be happy-go-lucky and thick skinned. The dour ones usually didn't get much help from the passengers when it came to having the fare ready or moving on or off the bus smartly so as to keep time. There were some who went by the book, in those days the buses were very much run along the lines of the military.

Wellingborough and Corby, were very working class and most people really watched the fares, but Corby seemed to have a lot of Scots working in the town and their attitude towards the fares was to avoid paying anything at all.

There was a particular working men's club where a huge mob used to crowd on board and the first passenger had no change and made an issue of paying, by the time you had sorted him out everyone was getting off without paying. A driver said to me that we ought to fix them and on leaving the club stop he stalled the bus, then couldn't get it started, when he did it was kangaroo stalls.

Eventually I got all the fares in and when we did reach their stop they were most annoyed and ranting on about the pathetic driving skills from up front, I rang us off and we roared away with the men shouting abuse after us, luckily I didn't have to do that run again. But this is typical of the sort of little dramas that made the job so enjoyable.

There were always awkward passengers but violent ones were the exception, it was not a problem in the 60s like today, I suppose it was all very gentlemanly then, a passenger with a grievance may invite you to step of the bus and settle it behind the bus shelter, etc. This happened to me once, as he stepped off expecting me to follow, I closed the doors and drove away. But really we didn't seem to have to get involved with making out reports for the company, most disputes got settled at the time, but there were always fare disputes and my response to the person was take it to the company as they set the policy.

Early running also used to upset passengers, the county runs were very slackly timed and when we got used to who was likely to be waiting for the bus, if they were not there it was a case of not bothering to hang around, this applied especially to the last bus of the night, after we had dropped off the final passenger on the way to some village it was a case of turn around and head back as quick as we could.

One passenger who had complained about early running found me ready for him the next time as I had put my watch forward and he refused to accept that it was correct, on arrival at Derngate he spoke to the inspector who asked to see my watch, of course it was now showing the correct time, the next week and on the same trip, the driver who was a regular was not at all pleased about being asked to keep to the timetable.

The management seemed to keep a low profile and leave it all to the inspectors. A good inspector really worked with the crews to see that the company provided a good service to the public, the crews respected this, unfortunately, the bad eggs in the ranks only incited the RSM types to really make it difficult for everyone, however most inspectors let you get on with the job as long as you were doing your best, the secret was not to attract attention to yourself. But the Blakey's really did get given a hard time by the crews, there were always plenty of Stan and Jacks about – stereotypes from a popular comedy TV series 'On the Buses'.

There was a certain amount of animosity against the part-timers as not all staff agreed with the policy, but for the crews that wanted Saturdays off on a regular basis it was a godsend. Full-timers were not threatened in any way regarding loss of income as the plan to employ PTs would have been withdrawn immediately at the sign of any union trouble. As a part-time driver I did come across the odd occasion that a full-time conductor balked at working with me, but this was not a general feeling and the company did its best to assign two PTs together as a crew on a regular basis.

We drove anything that the company had except for buses equipped for OMO (one-man operation), the regular men expected the part-timers to have the oldest stock but this didn't

A classic view of a traditional Tilling single-decker, as number 431 climbs away from Kettering depot on a short working Kettering–Corby service 256. The full service was the lengthy Northampton–Stamford. CNH 865 was new in 1952 – originally with a 6-cylinder Bristol engine, a 5LW was fitted in 1957. Note the attractive dual-purpose seats. (R.H.G. Simpson)

Number 805, a Bristol K6B, new in 1950, heads north out of Bedford. The Clapham on the screen refers to a small village, now a suburb of Bedford, on the A6, not the famous railway junction in south-west London! (R.H.G. Simpson)

always work out and on one occasion we were rostered a brand new FLF, I thought I was in heaven, but questions were asked later as to why we got the bus given to us.

Of course then the standard buses for part-timers were K, KSW, LD, FS, L and occasionally the MW, the latter were not all that common for PT work, I preferred the FS over the LD, we didn't get FLF too much but really I didn't mind the Ks at all, I rather liked them, the vision from the cab was much better than an LD and I found the seating position much more comfortable. All of course were crash gearboxes at that time but really once the art was mastered it was nothing to worry about plus I was younger then and heavier steering on some of the types didn't bother me either.

I recall it was the ex-ENOC L types, some of them had rough gearboxes by then and I was always careful to make sure I was in the right gear when ascending or descending hills, I once came to a full stop on a hill and then had to sort the box out, this was with an L and I can still hear all the cheering from the passengers as we finally pulled away up the hill, I was too embarrassed to turn around and acknowledge them.

The roads were really quiet in comparison to today, the only place John Royle would encounter any congestion was in Northampton and it was never tailbacks, just more traffic. The county routes were very quiet for car traffic and never a problem for the buses, and John traversed some narrow lanes along his way. He said that he always seemed to have all the time in the world, the timetable was most generous.

His shifts were those that the regular men didn't want, those available and the worst would have been the aforementioned runs into the Wellingborough, Kettering, Corby area. Nowhere was particularly rough in the mid-60s, most of the problem in Northampton. On a Saturday evening was just all the lads in the pubs, when a lot of the villagers would come into town and it seemed to be rivalry amongst themselves or with the Northampton lads. Also then, there didn't seem to be many of what we would call immigrant minorities. Everyone was local and indeed many people used the term of 'Me ducks' when addressing strangers. London overspill in towns always seemed to generate problems.

Bus maintenance was very good, it wasn't very often that John or anyone else had need to write up a bus on the defect sheet at the end of the day. Everything usually seemed to work and the buses were always kept tidy and clean. John Royle said crews were sometimes envious of other depot's buses, having the misconception that they must have better stock than Northampton. With the central works in town it was common practice for buses out shopped to be used in service for a week or so before being sent back to their home depot. All they did was put up a route number and a blank destination. John remembers a crew 'having a bus I think was based at Luton and while it was on the bay, facing out, someone put up Diagnostic Centre. Out went the bus and after a while of being called doctor or some other medical term by the passengers the conductor went around and checked the front. We always seemed to have some good laughs on the buses in those days.'

Stony Stratford was well linked to Wolverton in the 1960s, where the main employer was the railway workshops in the town. Wolverton, with its terraced houses and mean-looking streets, looked like somewhere dropped down from Lancashire. It may have been the general attitude of the unionised railway artisans that reflected on the local buses as well. Bletchley had a fair number of Londoners at their depot. This caused some friction between the garages – compounded when both groups were forced together when the garages were amalgamated at Winterhill in Milton Keynes. Bill Horwood recalled the steady changes taking place through the span of the 1960s. He said:

> I bought my house in New Duston in 1962. As a skilled man working at UCOC Main Works, I was earning £14 5 shillings and 9 pennies for 40 hours work. The house cost £2,250 and I remember toting my pay slip around the building societies. My wife was earning £6 a week in a clothing factory.
>
> As I moved up the ladder in my job, to charge hand, foreman and then body shop superintendent, I became piggy in the middle. I remember telling the old chap next door, when I took the charge hand's job. He said it was the worst thing, I'd lose all my mates and the folk at the top wouldn't want to know me as one of them – they'd look on me as a peasant. Never join management, he said. They manipulate you. He was right. I had enjoyed my job up until then. Promotion put me at the point where the pressure meets. On the shop floor, your mates are your mates. Put on a smock and it all changes.

The Oxford–Cambridge line would have been closed earlier but for the difficulty of finding crews to man the proposed jointly operated United Counties (Tilling) and City of Oxford (BET) replacement buses. The proof of this particular pudding was a steadily declining service that had petered out before mid-1980s deregulation. The service was chronically unreliable, drivers indifferent and sometimes off route. Thus the MPs words were prophetic. City of Oxford soon relinquished their involvement and by the late 1970s, cancellations without notice from UCOC were commonplace. Inevitably, the service went the same way as UCOC's Bedford–Oxford operation.

City of Oxford driver Ron Naylor used to cover the latter route, jointly operated with UCOC, which was established during the 1930s. He recalled the fuss Chief Inspector Dunlop would make if everything was not up to scratch. Fortunately Oxford used AEC vehicles. This company, AEC, had evolved to meet the heavy demands of the capital's transport system. They were designing a chassis complete with pre-selector gear box and air brakes way back in 1933; it was the RT. It featured a massive 9.6 litre diesel engine, driving a fluid fly wheel, with the gear lever in a gate and a slightly higher driving position than a Regent type. Oxford ran a large fleet of AEC Regents. Pre-war models used a single plate clutch, with the drive line to the near side of the chassis, and a 7.4 litre engine. Post-war models were much the same, using a triple servo braking system and a 7.58 litre engine linked to a four-speed crash gear box. City of Oxford bought twenty and Ron Naylor recalled the effort of so many gear changes on the Oxford–Bedford run.

The predecessor of the UCOC/City of Oxford service between Bedford and Oxford was operated by Bedford Blue Coaches twice daily: out at 9.00 a.m. to Oxford, back to Buckingham at noon, and then to Bedford. They returned to Buckingham at 4.00 p.m. where the company based a small feeder coach to connect with Stony Stratford – a link picked up when UCOC established their Stony Stafford depot – now a tyre fitter's. Bert Woodfield was the driver. He recalled: 'I kept the coach in a little garage along the Tingewick Road. They used to keep a Shell petrol tanker there as well. Mr Gammon owned the business and his daughter collected fares on the Oxford–Bedford run. I was only earning just over £2 a week just before the war, June 1939. I told Mr Gammon I was going to drive for the London Brick Co. at Calvert. 'A dirty job', he said. I said 'I know, but it's clean money'.

The Transport Holding Co. had taken over from the British Transport Commission in 1962. Life for UCOC and other Tilling companies remained much the same. As we noted previously, railway companies had protected themselves by taking share holdings in the group. These were separated out upon the creation of the state-run British Railways (BR) in 1948. To the idealists of Harold Wilson's 1964 Labour Government, a properly formed National Bus Co. would be a natural partner for BR. The groundwork had been done years ago. Barbara Castle set upon her mission with zest. Small operators like Red Rover suffered from a decision to cut the 50 per cent subsidy on new vehicles unless they were adaptable to one-man operation. Red Rover resolved the problem by ordering new, luxury, Plaxton-bodied Leyland and AEC chassis for dual service and Keith coach operation, gradually replacing a motley collection of AECs.

All major bus companies were destined for state ownership, with the local exceptions of Northampton and Luton Corporation Transport systems. The move to get rid of bus conductors and the old camaraderie immortalised by Stan and Jack in television's *On the Buses* was well under way. One-man operation on single-deckers had been commonplace early in the decade. The modern, rear-engine, front-entrance double-decker set the standard across the board. Smaller companies like Red Rover, using down-graded Keith Coaches and later new dual-purpose vehicles, could present heavily laden shoppers and older passengers with quite a problem climbing up steps to get on board. Yet legislation to allow access for all was a long way off. What companies like Red Rover and Wesleys lacked in amenities they made up for in offering regular staff on local routes, in contrast to UCOC and City of Oxford. Their staff were usually part of the local scene, often enjoying the same gossip as their passengers and a bit of a lark.

Parcel delivery was an idea developed by the UCOC. Buckingham ironmonger Frank Markham recalled: 'When there used to be a regular bus service to Oxford, Banbury and Northampton, my uncle started a bus parcels service. Anyone with an urgent parcel for anywhere along those routes used it. We had an official United Counties or Midland Red stamp and the conductor would collect it. That's how I was introduced to National Travel. They wanted an agent to sell tickets and they asked the United Counties controller to recommend someone. He said that since Markhams already looked after their parcels and they could probably organise the tickets and so his business grew. The Associated Motorways express coach from Cheltenham to Yarmouth used to run through Buckingham in those days.

As the 1960s moved on, the stalwart Ks were inevitably confined to local work. One regular young passenger on the 346 route recalled the 1960s, when he opened the window down to feel the summer breeze and pretended that he was flying.

With the roof of Kettering Garage in the background, 919 climbs the steep hill of Northampton Road into Kettering's town centre. An elderly couple march with equal determination alongside this KSW5G bus, which was new in 1952. (R.H.G. Simpson)

A handsome, long, low FLF6B, number 619, stands in Luton bus station, waiting to move westward on service 61 to Aylesbury. It was one of twenty-four (617–640) bought between 1961 and 1963. On its other side stands a Luton Corporation Leyland on service 6 to Dunstable. (R.H.G. Simpson)

Waiting in front of the library, on Kettering Town Service 292, in Sheep Street, Kettering, is 403. It is an LWL6B with an 8ft wide ECW body, seating thirty-nine and new in 1951. (R.H.G. Simpson)

This KSW6B fifty-six-seater, fleet number 863, is heading east out of Dunstable on a sunny Saturday, passing a stylish Ford Zodiac convertible parked on the right – a symbol of the affluent modern motorist – and is replete with lady passenger fresh from the hairdressers. A cool conductor grips the back platform rail, surveying the scene and maybe thinks of youthful pleasures to follow that evening. (R.H.G. Simpson)

Derngate bus station, mid-1960s, a scene of tribal excitement on Saturday nights, but otherwise plenty of room to manoeuvre the buses. (John Royle)

It was always fast along the long straight between Granborough and Oving. I remember these girls in tight tops, pencil skirts and bouffant hairstyles getting on, smelling of perfume and all made up, giggling and gossiping. There was so much hair spray on their back-combed hair, they looked like they'd had a fright. They gave me a funny look. Then up comes the conductor, a young one, his hair slicked down with Brylcream. I'd watched him combing it when we got on in Winslow High Street. He was soon upstairs after the girls, giving them the old Jimmy Dean look. Serious words were exchanged, 'Yeah, course I will love', he said, moving my way to shut my window without so much as a by-your-leave. After all, he couldn't have them arriving in Aylesbury's pleasure parlours or the queue for the Granada cinema looking less than perfect. It was all part of the service.

Initially BET resisted Government overtures to join Tilling under the Transport Holding Company (THC), but they eventually signed, thus facilitating the 1968 Transport Act and the means of establishing the National Bus Co. One result was a directive for new liveries; apple green with a white band or poppy red with a white band. The green was not dissimilar from the existing UCOC green. The visual effects were more drastic upon Luton Corporation buses, taken over by UCOC and having to go green like the rest.

At least Northamptonians could keep the bright red livery of their standardised Daimler/Roe rear-entrance double-deckers covering inner-town travel while UCOC plied away from Northampton on the major inter-county routes beyond. Frank W.A Johnson, probably the longest serving UCOC driver had to put up with his wife nagging him that he would be better off working for Northampton Corporation Transport because at least he would get a pension. His daughter, Dawn Rush, recalled how much he enjoyed his job, starting in the 1920s and winning regular safe driving awards. Working on his allotment in St Andrew's Road, Northampton was his main relaxation and Dawn said: 'You could set your watch by him.' He retired aged seventy, enjoying twenty-seven years of retirement.

The long established coach services of Birch Brothers had been taken over by UCOC in 1969. The brothers had been pioneers from the horse-bus days of London. Their main service from Rushden to Bedford and King's Cross had used double-deckers with large luggage capacity because it passed the gates of RAF Henlow and was much used by

Bus number 426, part of Stony Stratford's allocation and one of six SC4LK Bristol chassis with ECW thirty-five-seat front entrance bodies developed for one-man operation. Although fitted with a vertical front engine, the driver could turn to attend to passengers fares. (R.H.G. Simpson)

Biggleswade market place with empty bus stands on a wet day. This Bristol KS5G, new in 1950 and seen here a few years later, has worked in from Hitchin. (R.H.G. Simpson)

National Servicemen in the late 1940s and 1950s. United Counties also became part of the National Travel Express group, leading to coaches being painted in a rather insipid white livery, relieved eventually by flashy bold alternate red and blue lettering, spelling the word National.

Number 941, a Luton-allocated KSW6B nears its destination, Luton Midland railway station on a Saturday afternoon in the early 1960s. (R.H.G. Simpson)

A Northampton allocation Bristol RE is waiting here at Eastbourne before taking holiday makers back to the East Midlands from fairly sunny East Sussex. An East Kent AEC stands alongside. Soon the passengers would be hurtling along the motorway, the REs being very fast vehicles, easily cruising at 70–75mph. The M of MX2 indicates M1 Motorway service. (RHG Simpson)

5

New Destinations

Labour came to power in 1964, in the wake of Tory sleaze. In the event we got more stop-go economics, trade-union rule and inflation. Not surprisingly, their plans for a grand new city were, in reality, no more than a massive London overspill exercise, with County Architect Fred Pooley's scheme for a car-free settlement binned by the expediency of Wilson's cash-strapped regime. Pooley was responding to the South East Economic Planning Council's mid-1960s plan. Local MP Robert Maxwell commented at the time: 'From what I have been able to gather of the financial and practical feasibility of the Pooley scheme I should be surprised if the Government were to decide in its favour.' It did not. His scheme for development in North Buckinghamshire envisaged a 23,000-acre city for 250,000 inhabitants. A monorail was intended to reduce dependence on the motor car, but Milton Keynes did not even get a railway station until 1982. All was in the hands of a feeble development corporation.

By May 1965, the county council had abandoned the proposed partnership with a Government which declined to guarantee any shortfall in funds that might result from lack of investment. With two depots in the designated new city area – Milton Keynes is not officially a city – United Counties were the major operator, although smaller companies like Wesley provided services. Indeed, in the 1950s Wesleys had operated the forerunner of them all with a Saturday service from Newport Pagnell to Milton Keynes village – the little place engulfed with others but privileged to offer up its name.

For years they had worked in partnership with United Counties, then in 1970, Luton Corporation sold out to United Counties in 1970. The business case for running their own buses was on the wane, along with the number of workers being ferried to the giant Vauxhall car plant in Kimpton Road. The United Counties fleet was thus boosted with a mixed bag of Dennis Lolines (a version of the Lodekka), Leyland Titans, Albion Lowlanders and more Bristol REs.

The Government's bus subsidy grant was launched in the name of efficiency rather than safe and stress-free working practices. They wanted ubiquitous one-man operation. AEC had been ahead of the game with the FRM1 the rear-engined double-decker was the future. Regent production ceased in 1968 with chassis 2MD3RA and delivered as a complete bus in 1969. But with little foresight AEC designed the Renown as a low height bus, with good inside headroom. Red Rover continued crew operations into the 1970s, covering themselves by buying subsidised coaches and using them on private hire and excursions. They bought a new Park Royal-bodied Renown in 1964, registration DPP990B and went on to buy five more ex-Nottingham with Weyman bodies, the last one still in service when the company was taken over in 1987.

Private companies and Corporations could not buy Bristol products by law. The company got around this by allowing Dennis to build them under licence and the concept was also copied by Albion. Dennis's version was called the 'Loline'. When Bristol built a forward entrance version, Dennis followed suit, the FLF was created – the second F referring to forward entrance. Throughout the 1960s United Counties bought large numbers of Lodekkas and inherited some Dennis Lolines when it acquired the Luton Corporation fleet in January 1970.

Bristol were no less radical in the single deck department, using the United States concept of engine mid-way and horizontal below the coach floor. Consequent LS and MW types became almost as ubiquitous as the Lodekkas on Nationalised bus routes. The company took matters a stage further with a chassis taking a rear engine mounted under the floor. The rear arrangement was made more compact by mounting the gear box ahead of a dropped centre rear axle. An air suspension prototype bus version was on the road in 1962, followed by a forty-seven-seater coach; with production getting under way the following year. Letters RE denoted the type with suffixes of LL and LH added according to whether the bus had a long low or long high frame. The design was an enormous success, and very well represented throughout the country.

Since 1969, Leyland held a 50 per cent share in Bristol, while National Bus owned the rest. In 1975 Bristol was revamped as Bristol Commercial Vehicles. With National bus in mind, Leyland named their new integral design the National, which ousted the indefatigable RE. Leyland took total control in 1982, along with Eastern Coachwork, paving the way for the inevitable demise of both companies before ultimately destroying itself. In the meantime the Leyland National Marks I and II proved moderately successful, though the heyday of bus travel seemed to be over and certainly not about to be saved by de-regulation.

Leyland had much to gain from the Bristol link. The latter had pushed double-deck development a stage further with the VR. Leyland may have had the concept first, usurping the AEC FRM1, but Bristol offered the first 36ft-long option. Visually similar to the Lodekkas by dint of coachwork and the same dropped centre double reduction rear axle, the 1966 prototype had a Gardner engine and was designated VRLL6G. The LL referred to long low frame, making it suitable for low bridges. A long rear overhang made it unpopular and it was not until the transverse-engined VRT, of 1969, that the type became commonplace – the short low frame VRT/SL at 30.5ft being the most popular.

The vehicle was perfect for one-man operation, with a semi or fully automatic gear box. Series 2 appeared in 1970 and Series 3 in 1974, the latter with a well insulated engine to cut noise. Series 3 added the option of Leyland engines to the standard Gardner. Total VRT production had reached 4,474 when it ended in 1981.

Right: Veteran and one of UCOC's safest drivers, Frank Johnson, pictured in the 1950s. His daughter Dawn said he loved his life on the buses and he was regularly given safe driving awards. He didn't need Gordon Brown to tell him not to retire until he was 70! (Dawn Rush)

Below: Luton's 282 stands in leafy Portsmouth before working X36 back to Hitchen. An independent Bedford/Willowbrook waits behind to work a duplicate back to Luton. TBD282G was new in May 1969, for the summer season, passing to the new Luton & District in January 1981. (R.H.G. Simpson)

Leyland and AEC had forged a marketing link in 1962, the former always having the world edge so that the AEC name was gradually diminished until the historic Southall works closed in May 1979. In 1969 Leyland foresaw the demise of the double-decker and saw no future in plying down country lanes. They wanted to build a city bus. Early 1970s NBC operations saw more former BET companies taking Bristol-ECW vehicles. Leyland took a 25 per cent stake in Bristol ECW in 1965, increasing to 50 per cent in 1969. The Leyland National Bus project would seal Bristol and ECW's fate.

A warm summer day as 146 Bristol MW dual-purpose saloon, new in 1960, heads out of Victoria for a run to the coast on X2 – wrongly shown on the screen as 2X. Its sister vehicle behind carries roof boards for reading Nottingham–Northampton–London, which was X1, but in this instance it was probably acting as a duplicate in the busy summer season. (R.H.G. Simpson)

Parked up in Thames Valley country, this is a dual-purpose forty-one-seater body on a LS5G chassis. Of 1957 vintage and nearly new when photographed, adding a splash of green among the red. The Thames Valley K type to the left offers the clue that this is taken at Reading because of the Earley, Winersh and Wokingham destinations displayed on the blind – but why would anyone want to go on an excursion to Reading? (R.H.G. Simpson)

Number 482 stands on lay over at Bedford bus station, splashed with winter mud and grime. New in February 1954, with a thirty-nine-seater coach body on an LS chassis, it was repainted into green and cream bus livery in 1964 and withdrawn in July 1973. The Cave Brown Cave heater system can be seen fitted to one of the Lodekkas behind, a bus ready to work the 143 trunk route whilst its sister Lodekka does a local run to Ampthill. (R.H.G. Simpson)

One of a batch of sixteen dual-purpose LS6B chassis-based buses, this is number 469, photographed at a wet Gloucester Green in the 1950s and heading for a hopefully sunnier Bournemouth. (R.H.G. Simpson)

A 1954 LS6B on a Luton town service in the early 1960s – the front wing of a locally built Vauxhall Cresta is just visible to the left and an older Vauxhall L type is coming along just behind the bicycle. The bus's door is open, indicating a sunny and warm day. (R.H.G. Simpson)

Passing across the top of Temple Square, Aylesbury, is 104, a 1956 LS5G with bus body, seating forty-five passengers – not much knee room in a 30ft long vehicle. It is Amersham bound, some 20 miles away and heading off Kingsbury Square – the new Friars bus station yet to open. Aylesbury was the most southerly UCOC depot and Amersham was on the edge of London's metro land and also reached by Thames Valley and London Transport. (R.H.G. Simpson)

An earlier view of 120, note the underlined fleet name on the green panel. The management celebrated the advent of the 'Swinging Sixties' by enlarging the letters and removing the line! This bus is on Saturday's Sunday Summer X24 to Luton, Portsmouth and Southsea.

This VR was photographed on 29 May 1972. Number 783 in the fleet, it had only been in service just over a month, as its traditional bright UCOC livery attests. Soon all new vehicles would appear in apple green with white relief on the double-deckers. This picture was taken at the garage, Bedford Road exit at UCOC's Northampton depot. (Andrew Shouler)

These two elderly battered red and cream Lodekkas stand in Houghton Road on 22 February 1973. UCOC paid Cumberland Motor Services £265 each for them, had them spray painted up into UCOC livery before giving them to the Stony Stratford depot. Their five-speed gear boxes did not get full use around the growing Milton Keynes district. (Andrew Shouler)

Formation of the National Bus Co. took uniformity a stage further in 1969, founding a joint Leyland and National Bus Co. business to develop the integral single-decker bus with export potential. For many years Bristol had a stranglehold on the British bus market with their Lodekkas, the perfect solution to low bridge and leafy lane navigation. Poor old AEC had done their best to compete through the Bridgemaster but there were not enough BET or independent takers to make it work.

Bill Horwood has no fond memories of the Leyland National which was foisted on his company. He said it was a noisy and difficult bus to work on. It was the only one he ever hated, explaining that:

> Panels were held on by Avdel rivets. We reckoned to have at least two buses in main works every week for repair. Trying to drill out those rivets finished the drill bits off as soon as you started trying to drill in the hole you'd punched. We didn't know that we had to have expensive Avdel drills, guns and cutters and the panes were so wide we had to remove seats to pull out the internal formica panels to cut the rivets from the inside.

Bill faced other problems when UCOC bought Luton Corporation in the early 1970s, taking over a motley collection of buses, in poor repair. Bill said: 'These scrap heaps started arriving for testing. They were falling apart and just about crippled our system. The Luton people were miffed we'd taken them over and wanted nothing to do with them. They said the buses were our problem now.' London Transport's country buses and Greenline services were running into the Luton and Aylesbury areas of United Counties' services and were also caught up in the changes. The 1968 Transport Act had not affected London, but separate legislation transferred control of London transport to the Greater London Council. Having no interest in the country operations, these were transferred to a new National Bus Co. subsidiary – the second largest, having over 1,300 vehicles, including some ancient but reliable fifty-six-seater RTs. The problem was that they needed a two-man crew and were expensive to run.

Many enthusiasts enjoyed the variety of liveries and vehicles throughout the express coach network, but the formation of the National Bus Co. (NBC) combined a number of independent operators under one roof. Efficiency and saving money would be a guiding principle, otherwise why bother? Some old routes, like Associated Motorways from Cheltenham to Norwich disappeared. In time National Express was privatised and moved into railway franchise, taking over services from Norwich Thorpe Station to Cambridge. From here, nowadays, passengers can transfer to the service run by Stagecoach United Counties, running through to Oxford.

Buses magazine reported in March 1984:

> The introduction of the latest National Express timetable on January 22nd brought with it the end of what is probably one of the most famous features of the coach industry; from the date the interchange facility at Cheltenham with its celebrated mass departure was abolished. Thus ended almost 50 years of coach history, the first such coach operation occurred in July 1934.

The old bus station became a car park.

Along with the NBC name, express services were re-branded National Express. New fleet names took a while to work through, but the distinctive white livery with large red and blue lettering was adorning a modern range of Plaxton bodied Leylands by 1972, though there was still a little room for individual company names.

Clearly, however, the private operator was not going to have much opportunity for growth alongside the Tilling subsidiary of UCOC. The lack of opportunity for competition, and the high levels of subsidy required for the state-owned concerns, were the major arguments in favour of de-regulation.

As housing developed in Milton Keynes, the Development Corporation required bus services to be run. These began on 1 November, 1971, running from Bletchley, via Fenny Stratford, along the Watling Street to Stony Stratford and Wolverton; and all for 18p return or 10p single – generously subsidised by the Corporation. The single-decker Bristol MWs were painted green and white, with the words 'Milton Keynes New City' on the waist rail. Routes gradually increased, numbered MK1 to 5 and 10, including service to the newly instituted Open University at Walton.

Dial-a-Bus was an innovation of March 1975, centred on Woughton, using six new Mercedes minibuses painted bright orange and yellow. These small vehicles could penetrate the estates and use minor roads – residential areas were not built with access for long-wheel-base coaches and double-deckers in mind – and so provide door-to-

Saturday morning, 20 July 1985, on Market Hill, Newport Pagnell and a York Bros Ford Plaxton Supreme – though still in Wesley livery – prepares to leave with their Northampton service 526. A UCOC Leyland National, 556 in the fleet, passes on the 425 to Renny Lodge Hospital before returning at 9.00 a.m. for Bletchley, via central Milton Keynes. It advertises 'City Rider 2 tickets at £4.40 per week and £16.50 per month'. (Andrew Shouler)

Aylesbury's 477 Leyland National stands on the Aylesbury market square, outside the historic county court house in the mid-1970s – judging by the girls' clothes and hairstyles. This building has been made famous recently as the location for the mythical Highfield Court House in the television series about Judge John Deed. The bus was new in June 1974 and this service was to Bedgrove. The driver seems to have gone missing and the young passenger looks bemused. (R.H.G. Simpson)

door service with a thirty-minute response time. Unfortunately the system suffered problems with reliability and finance. Buses were withdrawn in 1980.

Northampton grew concurrently with Milton Keynes, having its own Development Corporation to make sure that it did not lose out economically to Milton Keynes. The town had been included in the South East Economic Planning Council's mid-1960s plan for four major swathes of development stretching away from London, aiming to make the greatest use of motorways and mainline railways existing or planned up to 1975.

The bulk of the region's growth was to be channelled into these areas. Northampton, like Milton Keynes, was identified as a major growth point. Luton was referred to in the plan as a study area but was booming due to the local motor industry and later airport expansion. There was going to be increasing scope for bus and coach traffic involving United Counties in particular. Northampton Corporation also became involved in new bus services, using one-man-operated single-deckers – female drivers were a rarity then – after years of using traditional open platform double-deckers allowing the convenience of hopping on and off at traffic lights, facilitating crime for those who didn't like to pay.

Out in the more northerly and rural parts of UCOC operations, the bus was still a vital link in the 1970s. Susan Harris, née Calver, recalled:

During the 1970s I lived two doors away from the last stop in Rushden, Northants on the Irchester Road. Every Wednesday my brother Stephen and I went to Wellingborough with mum to help Grandma and Grandad with the weekly shop which of course incorporated a trip to Wellingborough Market.

We always caught the bus around quarter past nine and if we'd been good, we children were allowed to ride on the top deck. I remember chasing around the bus stop driving mum mad while waiting impatiently for the bus to arrive and the excitement as we could see it coming from two hills away. Stephen and I would clamber onto the back of the bus, straight past the conductor and up the curly stairs which seemed massive, heading straight for the long seat while mum stayed down stairs.

It was great; we'd hold onto the silver bar in front of us, trying to perch our bums on the seat which was too far away. Once we were out of Rushden, we felt like we were flying on a big roller coaster down a great big hill, down into Knuston, cries of 'weeee…' hitting all the trees that over grew the road. It felt like we would never stop. But of course we had to get back up the other side. The bus driver changed gear and the bus roared its way back up into Irchester.

Every time we went through Irchester we were both amazed at how the bus got round the 90 degree turn in the village. Every time, it seemed as if we would go ploughing through the lovely stone built cottages that faced us, along with the view of Irchester country park gorge. From the top deck it was amazing. During this period dad worked for Gallays engineering, on one of the industrial estates opposite the Dog and Duck on the London Road in Wellingborough. We always made a point of waving at dad as we went past even though we knew he couldn't see us.

Though buses could still give so much fun to children, bus companies were well in decline by the 1970s. As the late Ellen Powell of Simpson Village told United Counties, by letter in November 1973:

Too few people use the buses. May I suggest that this situation can arise from the difficulty experienced by newcomers and visitors in finding their way to the appropriate bus stop. This seems to be the case in Simpson Village. The 324 service (Northampton–Bletchley) is scheduled to stop at Simpson cross roads. The bus stop and bus shelter are midway between two road junctions (there are no true cross roads in the village). This stop is fine for passengers to Bletchley. Should one wish to travel from Simpson to Newport Pagnell, one has to leave the above stop, proceed to the cross roads... and walk along the Bletchley Road (i.e. in the opposite direction to Newport Pagnell) in order to find the bus stop. According to the timetable, one is still at Simpson Cross Roads.

The 17.21 Simpson – Fenny Stratford only service, Saturdays only, turns in front of the church midway between the two above stops. To wait at the bus shelter usually means missing this bus as it leaves almost immediately after turning.

The MK10 service (Wavendon Tower–Bletchley) is shown on the same timetable as stopping at Simpson Bridge. The bridge over the river, within sight of the timetable, bears the following inscription: BUCKS CC SIMPSON BRIDGE, BUILT 1930 on a large plaque. One might be forgiven for thinking the MK10 stops there. Not so.

In order to travel to Bletchley on this service, one has to proceed to the cross roads...take the old Newport Pagnell road for approximately a quarter mile, in the opposite direction to Bletchley and marked as a no through road, then turn up a steep right hand path on to the exposed heights of the H9 road. One has then arrived at the bus stop for Bletchley.

To travel to Wavenden, one takes a left hand turn over the old canal bridge, through an opening in the fence, under the new canal bridge, up a flight of steps, and again one arrives at the appropriate stop.

There is no indication on any of the stops to show which service uses that particular route.

Would it be possible to attach a simple sketch map to the public timetable in Simpson Village showing the stops with terminal points?

The seventies were a turning point for UCOC country and the nation as a whole. The local engineering tradition along with iron and steel working was set for rapid decline. In Northampton shoe making faced cheap foreign competition. A new breed of service workers would populate much of the area by the mid-1980s and most would want cars to drive to and from the sprawling housing estates. Northampton grew apace and the centre underwent massive redevelopment. Old neighbourhoods were bulldozed.

Nowadays modest market towns like Northampton are jamming up. Writer Jeremy Seabrook commented back in the 1970s when it was being re-developed:

During 1971 and 1972, the expansion of Northampton became for me a symbol of the new culture, tyrannical and inexorable in its compulsions... a more subtle and less readily observable bondage. (Jeremy Seabrook, *The Everlasting Feast*).

Seabrook went on to describe all the demolition required to make way for new dual carriageways as treating traffic like a vital 'cosmic menstrual flow'. He wrote:

> The line of the new urban expressway is announced: it passes through the most densely populated area of the town and will demolish a thousand homes, the abodes of the powerless and the poor... When challenged on the line of the road, the Chairman of the Highways Committee admitted that it had been designed to avoid the properties of the great employers of labour. (*The Everlasting Feast* p 213)

Northampton's Grovesnor Centre was constructed during the early 1970s and a new bus/coach station was incorporated. It opened in May 1976 and the former Derngate bus station, which had served the town for forty years, was demolished. The present Derngate Theatre and Arts Centre was built on the site.

The major change in bus station design was the idea of putting them undercover with convenient links to shopping centres. Concrete was a favoured building material because it could be easily moulded, was cheap and looked clean. But concrete fades, crumbles, gets dirty and these days does not get cleaned. Unlike stone, which it apes, it does not carry grime well. Not surprisingly there are talks and tentative plans between council and landlords, Legal and General, to re-develop the Greyfriars site. Nothing has been decided but the bus station's future is in doubt and an extended shopping centre under consideration.

When the sun is shining, you cannot beat an open-air bus station. However, consideration has to be made to Britain's uncertain weather. Peterborough struck a balance when they retired Bishops Road bus station, creating a covered bus station looking through glass at the open air, and attached to one of the best-looking shopping centres in Britain. It can be done. In Windsor, where tourism is paramount, there is a very pleasant coach park behind the truncated and decimated railway station – almost entirely obliterated by a frivolous shopping centre – and next to the river. It is a most pleasant spot in summer. ECW outlived Bristol for a while, making bodies for the Leyland Olympian, but demand for conventional buses was falling as operators tried to balance books by choosing minibuses with van-like bodies. Leyland were losing money. Production of Olympian bodies was transferred to Workington. The last job for ECW at Lowestoft, before closure in 1987, was to body the Olympian chassis for London Buses.

Milton Keynes City planners were not going to be left out of the running when it came to a status-symbol bus station. Estimating that 250 buses would be required for daily services, it was decided to close the Bletchley and Stony Stafford depots and open a state-of-the-art facility at Winterhill on 1 March 1983. The bus station was another palatial establishment, but even more so. Complete with granite and marble cladding, it opened on 27 May 1983.

In theory it made sense to site the new bus station near the railway station to facilitate an interchange. In reality it should have been nearer to the shopping centre, over half a mile east atop a hill – in a perfect world the centre would have been built nearer the

The view from the top of Northamptonshire County Council offices, toward the east end of Greyfriars bus station in Northampton, 28 September 1978. A Northampton transport VRT with Alexander bodywork is emerging past a traditional open platform Daimler Roe. To the far right a UCOC VRT/ECW is passing east along Lady's Lane. (Andrew Shouler)

railway line! Not surprisingly the bus station was never fully utilised, today appearing almost desolate and deserted, and looking like Lenin's mausoleum. National Express coaches call at MK Coachway, a grandiloquent title for a collection of unprepossessing pre-fabricated buildings. Waiting for buses on the draughty windswept station square is not an experience to be savoured from the authors' experience.

In spite of all the challenges, independent companies soldiered on. Car ownership had been increasing rapidly with drastic effects on revenue. Companies like Wesley and Soul's had seen the benefits of involvement in car dealerships, while the bread and butter of bus operations lay with the school runs in an age of increasingly centralised and enlarged school campuses. United Counties and the rest of the nationalised bus companies appeared little changed. Tilling companies had long been conspicuous through use of standardised vehicles.

Suddenly there was a style change in the form of Leyland Atlantean double-deckers and Leyland National singles. The good old RF, a common sight parked in Aylesbury's Buckingham Road, also disappeared from the Greenline front line. New Greenline coaches were Plaxton- and Duple-bodied, similar to the National Express types that added a new uniformity, displacing so much eccentricity and character of earlier years.

The biggest change followed Margaret Thatcher's and the Tory victory in the 1979 General Election. Thatcher and her mentor Sir Keith Joseph were no fans of trade

Just arrived at the arid desert of Milton Keynes bus station, in the summer of 1983, is Bedford allocation 584 Leyland National, new in 1978. It had worked in from Letchworth via Hitchin, Luton and Dunstable, having left Letchworth at 9.20 a.m. (Andrew Shouler)

unions or state enterprise, seeing the latter as a contradiction in terms. From now on industry was going to have to be leaner and fitter. Anything owned by the state, the Government decreed, should weather, and wither if need be, in the rough world of free competition.

The Road Traffic Licensing system underwent its first reform since inception in 1930, allowing competition on the National Express network, though passengers preferred to stay with a well-organised and recognisable system. On the vehicle front, a Leyland National type 2 offered more power and the Leyland Olympian replaced production of the Bristol VRT, a once great name.

By 1982 Leyland National was the major choice of the National Bus Co. Yet with overall passenger demand on the wane out of town, it was also the age of mini- and midi-buses. In 1985 the Government decided to rescind the nationalising act. Thus by the following year, the larger subsidiaries were breaking up. United Counties was split into three operating units: 1. Northampton, Kettering, Wellingborough, Huntingdon and Bedford areas, still called United Counties; 2. Luton, Aylesbury and Hitchin areas, called Luton & District Transport; 3. Milton Keynes area, called Milton Keynes City Bus. The counties were 'disunited' at a stroke.

In the extreme south of our region the old name of Red Rose, seen on the Aylesbury–Wendover route until Eastern National took it over, was resurrected in name,

Photographed at Oxford's Gloucester Green, on private hire, is number 251, an RE, displaying its 36ft length and chromium-plated bumper and wheel caps. (R.H.G. Simpson)

An interesting view at Houghton Road, courtesy of the depot engineer in 1973. On the left, Trent's Tiger Cub with Alexander forty-one-seat body, and one of six on hire to UCOC because of vehicle shortage. Next in line is an ex-Cumberland Lodekka bought for spares or possible re-certification and then two KSWs awaiting conversion to driver tuition. (Andrew Shouler)

Working a heavily loaded duplicate (relief) coach on the X22 Luton Bournemouth service is 481, a 1953 LS5G forty-one-seat dual-purpose vehicle. The two Duple SB coaches following behind were probably on hire to UCOC for the summer Saturdays – these weekends put considerable strain on the coach fleet, particularly during the holiday fortnight of late July and early August. (R.H.G. Simpson)

using the livery of recently demised Red Rover on their minibus fleet. They filled a gap, alongside Luton & District, who for a while continued the Red Rover name on a few selected vehicles. The new de-nationalised companies began operations on 1 January 1985. The former United Counties bus and coach fleet was reduced from 520 to just 263 for the new United Counties. Luton & District took over 193 and Milton Keynes City Bus had 64.

New liveries came into force with United Counties opting for a dark green with orange and cream half arrowhead stripe for buses and white blue grey stripe for coaches. Luton & District chose a traditional bright red and cream, recalling the red of former Luton days, while MK City Bus chose a rather insipid white and grey livery. In the west of the old United Counties region, City of Oxford, was sold to Arthur Townsend's management team on 15 January 1987. This company decided to retain the old National Bus Co. poppy red which had replaced their historic and more distinctive red and black in the 1970s. The name was changed to Oxford Bus Co. Divided from its South Midland operations since June 1984, services were confined to the city and London Citylink.

The 1980s saw the first major reform of bus legislation since the 1930s when ten Traffic Commissioners had been created. Those commissioners had been given authority to grant all relevant bus operator and driving licences in their areas. Licences tended to go to the established firms. Many years earlier the Great Western Railway had to sacrifice routes into Slough to Thames Valley. They also had a lucrative route between Oxford and Cheltenham.

Sister MWs at Victoria in the early 1960s. Number 145 carefully reverses in to unload its Nottingham passengers into the metropolis while 149 waits to whisk its load up the M1 to Leicester. New in June 1960, 145 was sold in November 1975. Number 149 was new in July 1962. Converted to bus seats and livery it lasted until September 1977. (R.H.G. Simpson)

The very first of the illustrious 250FRP, ready to work the X6 county route north of St Albans, Luton, Woburn and Northampton, 250 waits at Victoria with an MW at the rear, probably working the MX1 250. These REs were fitted with rear-mounted Gardner 6HLX engines. New in 1964, it was soon followed by 251FRP. (R.H.G. Simpson)

The Conservative Party's emotional hostility to a nationalised bus network can be gleaned from Michael Heseltine's memoirs, where on pages 112–113 he refers to the 1968 Labour Transport Bill. Rather critically he mentions local authorities who loved their municipal transport undertakings as if they were their offspring, with 'prominent' councillors chairing transport committees, and public service vehicles travelling about displaying municipal coats of arms, or gleaming liveries.

The long-awaited – and for some, the long-feared – de-regulation day dawned on 26 October 1986. Now smaller firms could get a bit more of the action. York Brothers had already given notice of running services to Daventry, Wellingborough and Irthlingborough from Northampton at lower fares than United Counties. These routes were additional to Yorks' Milton Keynes–Northampton service. United Counties responded by cutting fares on their competing service, extending their Wolverton service to central Milton Keynes. Other independents also introduced services, mostly short-lived, and the tussle between Yorks and United Counties was finally resolved by United Counties taking over Yorks' routes, except to Milton Keynes, in November 1988.

Keith Garages had taken over Red Rover in 1955. They had no intention of using 1980s deregulation to gain the sort of fortune Brian Souter and his sister were going to make out of Stagecoach and the old United Counties operation. Keiths had other plans, quitting the bus and coach business. Plans to sell out to Luton & District, successors to United Counties in the Luton and Aylesbury areas, through management buy out were being discussed in the local press the following December. Luton & District were assuring Red Rover employees that they would keep their jobs. The climate then was difficult, with a spate of take-overs as routes were opened to free competition.

An interesting addition to the fray was Peter Legg's 'little man's' public transport service, offering cheaper fares than the big boys, on the Aylesbury to Leighton Buzzard weekend route. A declared bus enthusiast, he chose a twenty-three-year-old ex-London Transport Routemaster – not surprising considering his weekday job with London Regional Transport!

Mid-1980s de-regulation dismembered the National Bus Co. Luton and Aylesbury operations would not last long. To some, this Thatcherite legislation appeared to be a recipe for disuniting the counties, harking back to the cut-throat days of pirate bus services and dubious standards, a move back to an age of seat-of-the-pants driving when people knew no better. It was tearing up years of hard work and progress, consolidating Britain's reputation that for all its dreams of integrated transport policy, the buccaneer's spirit and desire for a fast buck would once again come first, while public service came last.

The sibling success story of Ann Gloag and Brian Souter – having started a minibus and old double-decker service running Scottish miners to work, using perfectly good, cheap ex-London Routemasters – was a remarkable outcome of the process and was of great significance for United Counties. However, there was not going to be room for too many Gloag Souter-type operators in Thatcher's brave new world of public transport. More of the old pioneers, like Wesleys, were ready to retire, giving another Northampton independent the chance to expand. Wesleys became part of the York empire in May 1979.

Oldies like this elegant Bristol RE had been pensioned off a few years before de-regulation and such images evoke the elegance and individuality of a bygone age. This bus was not designed in a wind tunnel and its lines are nicely adorned with a script style fleet name. The flamboyant style of Aldershot is displayed on the bus adjacent. (R.H.G. Simpson)

Rolling slightly as it turns from Park Lane by Marble Arch, 254 seems devoid of passengers. The destination blind indicates that it will gain the M1 at Staples Corner and hurry up to Northampton before heading north-east to Corby. (R.H.G. Simpson)

In 1981 United Counties had been operating 500 buses, each one travelling 42,000 miles per year, a distance equal to 840 times around the globe, using 21 million gallons of fuel, carrying 5.3 million passengers and providing 1,850 jobs. The average operational life of each bus was said to be 10–15 years.

It takes a special talent to make money out of buses, especially today when the car maker and salesman must have their way. On 21 August 1990, Luton & District used the *Herald and Post* newspaper to announce celebrations of their third anniversary. They proudly informed readers that they had further expanded by buying Stevenage Bus and had a dedicated school bus fleet. Luton & District's chief executive, Graham Cunningham recalled the blisteringly hot day in 1987 when, after months of negotiation, the company was finally acquired from the National Bus Co. He said, 'We drove out of London in a "Hoppastopper" minibus, with a profound feeling of elation mixed with a sense of awe at what we had taken on. Bus travel had been in steady decline in the years leading up to privatisation and the fleet was rundown, engineering facilities were poor and morale low.'

Passenger complaints were the only area of growth. Luton & District gave every employee the incentive to support the company by giving them shares, but in a society obsessed with motor car status symbols, where latest models and number plates are the driving force, a more long-term attitude to transport is hard to establish. At the time of the Luton & District workers' buy-out of division of the old United Counties, there was a lot of optimism.

Managing Director Graham Cunningham, who had started his career with United Counties as a driver in 1975, told the *Buckinghamshire Herald* in September 1987, 'If I ask someone in the depot to do something, the chances are that I've done the job myself at some time'. He said he always remembers his time behind the wheel and aims to be as accessible as possible to the work force. 'If a driver knocks on my door, it means he thinks it's important and so it's important to me too.' He added that the company was not content to stand still and would expand into other fields.

Luton & District had their part of the old United Counties empire more or less to themselves, serving 400,000 around Aylesbury, Leighton Buzzard, Dunstable, Luton, Hitchin and Letchworth. Local identity fleet names such as Aylesbury Bus, Luton Bus and Hitchin Bus kept it personal looking. Aylesbury's United Counties Depot, built in Buckingham Road near the original Aylesbury Bus Co., had been a sub depot to Bedford – their allocated vehicles recognisable from blue fleet number plaques, with two vertical red stripes either side of the number. Painting Red Rover on the side of some of the buses was a pointless and short lived gesture. It could only have significance for bus enthusiasts and for enthusiasts the magic had gone. Who cares about enthusiasts anyway? Buses don't exist for them.

More successfully, Northampton Corporation established a separate company, Northampton Transport, to run their buses and extend routes. Sadly, the Government issued a directive that the company had to be offered for sale. United Counties responded with new routes and services to compete with Northampton Transport and both companies cut fares. Inevitably, the travelling public did not benefit for long

Towards the end of its life, Bristol RE number 273 stands at Oxford in full National White livery, working an express service to Northampton. The obligatory 'On Hire to National Express' sticker is in the windscreen behind the wiper arm. It and its five sub-class sisters were new in April 1968 and withdrawn in December 1982. (R.H.G. Simpson)

Two Bedford allocated vehicles, offering front end contrasts at Bedford bus station on 23 September 1972. MNV766 is LS5G number 107 with forty-five-seat bus body, new in 1956 and probably the oldest survivor of its class in service. The MW was new in 1962, a dual-purpose forty-one-seat body. Service 152 was Bedford–Kimbolton–St Neots. Service 204 was Welwyn–Bedford–Rushden – an ex-Birch Bros route. This 152 was on a short working, with the 13.40 Hitchin–Bedford. The VRT on the left is 781. (Andrew Shouler)

The long-established Birch Bros business was sold to UCOC on 14 September 1969 and included twelve Leyland Leopard coaches, fitted with various types of body. Shown here is 91FXD, with handsome Park Royal forty-nine-seater bodies on the 203M (motorway) London service to King's Cross. It became 191 in UCOC stock and lasted until 1974 – being new to Birch in 1963. (R.H.G. Simpson)

from this bus war as GRT of Aberdeen bought Northampton Transport, adding to the town's Scottish flavour – since Stagecoach had headquarters in Perth. Though a British invention, the name stagecoach conjures up images of the Wild West, gun law and the survival of the fittest. The Stagecoach bus company were certainly going to be trail blazers for the next ten years.

Toddington Garage survived as an outpost for Luton. Minibuses were soon the order of the day, starting in Luton and proving very useful when MK City Bus withdrew Sunday services from May 1987. Luton & District were able to provide Buckinghamshire County Council with eighteen white Sherpas as a stopgap to make good the loss, its minibus programme proceeding on apace. The new company was also developing services along routes to Flitwick and Bedford and there was some optimism regarding the future.

Meanwhile, using new minibuses, United Counties set up 'Street Shuttle' services in St Neots, Kettering and Corby and the 'Coachlinks' system. The latter, as its name suggests, aimed to provide a speedy, frequent service connecting towns and cities – from London in the south to Nottingham in the north, from Cambridge in the east, to Birmingham in the west, crossing at Bedford, offering a good choice of destination. Stagecoach Express services followed similar routes. In conjunction with Bedfordshire County Council UCOC hired two midi buses from Tricentrol for a trial period in September 1976. They were Ford A series with Tricentrol twenty-three-seater bodies, fleet numbers 71 and 72. They worked five routes in Leighton Buzzard, were well publicised

In the early 1970s Milton Keynes Development Corporation had one of their numerous bright ideas from transport in their new town. It centred on the village of Woughton, east of the centre, where residents could ring for a bus – a half-hourly response was expected. The idea was imported from the USA. When it started in March 1975, with six converted Mercedes vans, it was the largest system in the world outside North America. (R.H.G. Simpson)

UCOC Mercedes 309D, fleet number 7, with Charterway body, waits on Newport Pagnell, Market Hill, to work local service 135 north to Wolverton – note the Milton Keynes fleet name. It was photographed on 26 Octobert 1978. Along with number 8, it was new in February 1978 and withdrawn in May 1980. (Andrew Shouler)

and so popular that a third vehicle had to be hired over the Christmas period to meet demand.

De-regulation became more of a franchising business with outsiders bidding for routes, though encouraged to use National Express colours. In July 1986, there began a series of management buy-outs. Milton Keynes' Winterhill depot had the distinction of carrying the last major signage for the old National Express on the bus wash wall overlooking the west-coast main railway line.

Inevitably, new large groupings developed through a series of acquisitions. The notion of stimulating better and cheaper services through competition, aimed for by the 1985 legislation, started to appear at best naive. Luton & District Transport came into being in August 1987 when the National Bus Co. sold it to employees, setting a precedent for similar buy-outs in Derby and Clydesdale. Luton & District followed their Red Rover acquisition by buying more companies, the largest being London Country North-West, based in Watford and operating the former area of London Transport Country services.

In July 1994 Luton & District became part of the British Bus Group, receiving a new pale yellow and bright blue corporate livery in 1995, emblazoned with the operational name 'The Shires'. This title was at odds with the previously accepted use of the phrase which had been synonymous with the fox-hunting counties of Northamptonshire, Leicestershire and Rutland, not the suburbanised Home Counties of Bedfordshire, Buckinghamshire and Hertfordshire.

In the consolidation period that followed through the mid-1990s, British Bus was bought by the Cowie Group in August 1996. Cowie renamed itself 'Arriva', repainting vehicles turquoise blue with ivory front and side sweep, branding itself: 'Arriva serving the Shires'.

And so as the year 2000 approached, there were examples of all three major new groups in our old United Counties area – First Group being the largest and the owner of First Northampton, Arriva the second largest and Stagecoach, owners of United Counties.

Stagecoach were making major acquisitions nationwide. Bill Horwood's job had changed significantly by the time de-regulation made him redundant in 1986. He said:

> We had been tendering for a lot of out work, doing complicated bus conversions for clients like St John's Ambulance. I think the people at the top wanted deregulation. For a long time there was a view in the business that National Bus would get too big for itself and Maggie Thatcher was going to give the top people what they wanted. She carved it up amongst them. There was a time when money was no object. We soon felt their weight. They threw money at everything. You could almost say that as soon as National Bus came on the scene it was the beginning of the end.
>
> The work with all those complicated front and side plates for the corporate logo got very complicated. When it all changed we had a lot of enthusiasts around the works after destination blinds and route boxes. I don't know what they wanted them for, maybe they kept them in a shed and wound round to different destinations each day! I was glad to get out. Nowadays you don't see many old buses. The work is different. For some years I had

A Bristol VR fresh from Northampton main works in the late 1970s, carrying transfers all over, advertising National Holidays. (Bill Horwood)

Number 241, seen here at main works in the early 1980s. This vehicle is a Leyland Leopard with Willowbrook coach body, one of five new in 1980. It carries the special Greenline 760 livery for the Heathrow service. (Bill Horwood)

little hands-on involvement, spending a lot of my time dealing with equal opportunities issues, trade unions and other meetings.

For a while Bedford enjoyed the novelty of having eight ex-London Transport Routemaster double-deckers. Attractive, reliable, well suited to the United Counties livery and with the social benefit of old-fashioned conductors, they offered shorter pick-up times and speedier journeys. Success led to another eight vehicles being used in Corby.

For Milton Keynes during the late 1980s, the minibus predominated. A fleet of Mercedes vans, converted to carry twenty passengers, was an ugly contrast to the Routemasters of Bedford and Corby. Minibuses had become an increasing proportion of all National Bus Co. fleets by 1985, offering flexibility and reducing need for massive workshop/maintenance facilities. City Bus took over the independent Johnson's of Hanslope, thus gaining their Bletchley–Northampton route in competition with United Counties. The company bought some vintage Bristol VRs to run these services, which, even if not attractive to passengers, brought in the camera-laden enthusiasts and inspired a commercial video tape about 'Milton Keynes and its Bristols!' Another delight for the enthusiasts was a short-lived venture by a North London firm, R&I Coaches, who moved to Bleak Hall in the early 1990s. Here they established a business running trunk services from central Milton Keynes through Bletchley using minibuses, Leyland Nationals and ex-West Midlands double-deckers.

At this point the Bristol story had virtually ended. The VRs successor was a derivative of the Leyland Titan – which was not without Bristol influence – and would become known as the Leyland Olympian. The 1979 prototype was bodied at Eastern Coachworks. The last Bristol chassis was built in September 1983 – destined for Western National where there are still some shabby Bristol VRs rumbling and roaring about. The Bristol ECW combination which had been the hallmark and main load bearer of the Tilling operation until the demise of the National Bus Co. in 1988 came to an end.

Ex-London Routemaster in special green livery, number 708 in Bedford's allocation. This bus was new in April 1965 and to UCOC Stagecoach in January 1988, along with a further seven. With UCOC'S flair for publicity, the service was branded Routemaster and re-introduced conductor-operated services to Bedford and later, to Corby. Passengers appreciated the quick loading in town and the pleasure of riding on a Routemaster. Here 708 is working service 101 to Kempston – Williamson Road from Bedford town centre. Note the informative London-style blind. (Alan Henshall)

One of the authors recalls the gruelling ride from Cambridge to Bedford on the 128. Here, on 13 January 1973, VR number 790 waits to work the 15.10 forward to Northampton, having left Cambridge at 12.40 when photographed here at its home base in Bedford. It was only a few days in service when pictured here, and one of a group of five ordered by Eastern Counties and two by Eastern National. Owing to a vehicle shortage, UCOC took over the order. Note its black background number plate. All later vehicles were reflective. (Andrew Shouler)

6

DIFFERENT WORLD

Stagecoach, from its humble beginnings as little more than a family sideline, set the pace and standards for the post-de-regulation world. When the Government proposed that the same process of privatisation be applied to London's transport network, most private firms said it would 'not work'. Grey Green, the largest independent operator already working in London, said de-regulation would be disastrous for all London's commuters and have a seriously adverse effect on the economic life of the capital. In June 1991 it was reported that Grey Green, which had contributed to Tory Party funds, stated that commuters would face large fare increases and worse congestion, imposing untold misery on millions of London commuters for the sake of a redundant ideology. Stagecoach, a long time fan of London buses, showed no hesitation in buying in to the new system, when not surprisingly the Government ignored warnings and went full steam ahead, along with privatising plans for the British Rail, another attractive proposition for the rapidly expanding Stagecoach business.

On 10 October 1991, the *Bucks Herald* carried a report entitled 'Bus War Danger'. It reported the concerns of County Councillor Martyn Armour that a war was being waged on routes through Princess Risborough. Closer to the heart of United Counties affairs, Kettering bus station was sold to a developer in 1989 and a smaller facility opened in September 1989. The large garage and office premises occupied by United Counties in its heyday were now too large and a former car dealership site was bought off Rothersthorpe Road. MK City Bus were bought by Cambus of Cambridge in 1992 and in 1995 the MK Metro name was born. Cambus was bought by Stagecoach in 1995. By this time the Milton Keynes fleet was showing its age, the majority being well-worn Mercedes van conversions from 1986.

For a few heady months it seemed as if bus travel in Milton Keynes would revert to the glory days of green United Counties double-deckers, albeit with a few gaudy Stagecoach stripes. Rumours abounded as to just how many modern buses Stagecoach would introduce. By 1989, a little of the transport dust had settled, so much so that Gavin Booth was able to write, in the trade magazine *Buses* in February 1989's edition that 'business is picking up in the bus manufacturing industry, after the worst years the industry can remember'. He reported that Walter Alexander had boosted big bus

This could be seen as a symbolic image. Not quite the end of the road for RE number 252. Bill Horwood recalls his men got it roadworthy again, but the days of main works were numbered when this late 1970s picture was taken. (Bill Horwood)

Northampton's 232 in full National Livery, working route 487 to Nottingham in the early 1980s. A Leyland Leopard with Plaxton Supreme coach body, seating forty-nine, it was new in January 1979, passing to a dealer in October 1989, having been painted into white, blue and grey coach links livery in December 1986. The bored passengers look as if they would rather be on their way than stuck outside a café. (R.H.G. Simpson)

production to twelve a week, while Leyland increased Lynx production from two to twelve. Gavin Booth explained that orders were coming from ex-National Bus companies free from State control. New entrants to the business were moving away from costly old vehicles that they had started with, to new ones because it was cheaper in the long run. 'Only London Bus and Scottish Group were holding back', he wrote.

However, the Monopolies and Mergers Commission decided that the situation with Stagecoach and United Counties was against the public's interest, issuing a specific request for the Huntingdon district to be sold off together with Milton Keynes. The linking of these two divisions is hard to fathom because they are over 40 miles apart with no geographical or social connection.

Stagecoach had to agree, and in April 1997 the areas were sold off to a company headed by Mr Julian Peddle and called MK Metro. The Huntingdon operation used the name Premier Buses, subsequently being sold in 1997 to Blazefield. Meanwhile, MK Metro bought in new and nearly new vehicles, all painted an attractive deep yellow and blue. Services were reorganised and marketing introduced premier-route branding such as 'Easy Route 5'. On a wider front, the company began working with Milton Keynes Council on commercial and tendered routes.

The 1990s were testing times for bus operators. Dogma was everything to Central Government and matters were going to be compounded by a hasty and, many would say, botched railway privatisation. Sir Bob Reid, the last chairman of British Rail, told us that the railways had not been in better shape when he had to oversee privatisation. He said that if it had to be privatised, his board could offer a better model than the one chosen by Government – see *Not a Two Speed City* by Robert Cook. If the motive for private enterprise is to make a profit, it was difficult to understand why anyone would enter the fray as far as buses were concerned, not if they were going to keep up a comprehensive network.

Life in the bus lane was not easy. Newspapers were full of tales of trouble. MK Metro worked hard in the difficult environment of Milton Keynes, where problems were not specifically related to de-regulation. Had United Counties still been in charge, the difficulties would have been the same. A town designed for car ownership, with a sprawling central area, intricate little estate roads – arguably the biggest overspill development in Britain – combined with the traditional satellite areas of Bletchley, Wolverton, Stony Stratford and Newport Pagnell, not forgetting countless speed-restricting ramps and bumps, presents a major challenge. It says much for the company's efforts that patronage of the buses has increased 30 per cent over the past three years.

In June 1999 MK Metro became part of a newly formed Status Bus Group, with Julian Peddle as chairman and Steve Tilling as managing director. Burton's Coaches, Midland Choice, Telling's Golden Miller and The Londoners all came under the grouping; which differed from other large groups in that it is more of a co-operative between private member constituent companies, but affords such joint benefits as bulk vehicle and fuel purchase.

With New Labour coming to power in 1997, Deputy Prime Minister John Prescott also announced plans to expand into new fields – fields all over the south-east! His

Ex-UCOC Leyland Olympian/ECW photographed in Buckingham in May 1994. This bus was new in January 1982 and the penultimate of a group of twenty, dating from August 1981 to January 1982. Along with its eight sisters – 612–620 – it passed to Luton and District in December 1985. Here it carries the Aylesbury Bus brand livery of Luton & District on route 66 – part of the old UCOC 346 route. Jeffs service 32 hourly Bicester Oxford service is in the background – it fell victim to Stagecoach's inter-county Oxford Cambridge express. (Robert Cook)

Photographed in September 1991 in Buckingham Street, the former UCOC garage in Aylesbury's Buckingham Road, here carrying the banner of Luton & District, the new owners. The former enquiry office has become a charity shop. The Leyland National parked opposite is former UCOC 659. A Plaxton Paramount is parked on the garage forecourt. Both buses are in their new owners' bright red and cream relief livery. (Robert Cook)

controversial housing plan has been condemned as unsustainable. Whatever happens, it will have a major impact on the old UCOC stomping ground. It is a scheme for massive expansion of an already overcrowded south-east England. Though property speculators and developers are pleased, there are major implications for our overcrowded roads. It remains to be seen whether public transport can be sufficiently innovative to ease the inevitable increased congestion. Politicians seem to create endless problems for those involved in building, developing and operating buses. It is a battle between those who try to do a good job and those who make work for other people. Of course it would be unfair to ignore the sterling efforts of local authorities who see the problems at grass roots and strive hard to do something about them.

Solutions have included subsidised travel for employees and Park and Ride. Yet as long as cars are the British way to glamour and prestige, it is going to be an uphill struggle. The capital's mayor, Ken Livingstone, has a record of concern about the unglamorous yet vital issue of public transport. As GLC leader in the early 1980s, he initiated a 'Fares Fair' policy of subsidised travel throughout the London Transport network. Lord Chief Justice Denning ruled the scheme illegal. Now Livingstone has initiated congestion charges in his capacity as London's Mayor. Powerful forces endeavoured to block Livingstone's rise to power and smeared his efforts to free up the capital's roads, curiously in the name of freedom for the motorist. Interestingly, the scheme, introduced in February 2003, seems to be working. Politicians, having at first distanced themselves from congestion charges, are now talking about installing them in other conurbations.

A section of Peterborough's main multi-storey car park is named after Royce, apprenticed at the local railway engineering works and famous for the luxury limousines that bore his name. In Royce's day motoring was for the elite; it was left to Henry Ford to make it something for the masses. Yet that is how it is today. The fact that over 50,000 new cars went on to British roads just in the month of September 2003 ought to be a cause for concern to all.

One solution is to meet the motorist half-way with Park and Ride, but as Andrew Shouler observed: 'For many motorists it's a matter of honour to fight their car through the busy streets and win that parking place'. The Buckingham Society chairman and former deputy headteacher of the Royal Latin School, Edward Grimsdale, elaborated on the argument in the *Buckingham Advertiser* (7 July 2000). Commenting on the editor's remarks that a brave new world of better public transport, local shops and a cleaner environment with fewer cars would not happen overnight, Mr Grimsdale wrote: 'It will never happen unless people feel they must partially abandon their cars... The country won't receive neighbourhood shops as manna from heaven, but changes may be effected through the harsh laws of economics'.

In the most eastern reaches of the old UCOC empire, Cambridge – once a cloistered environment, affluent from academia, and tourism – avoided the extremes of grim side effects from industrial change. Now new homes and high-tech industry put strain on its infrastructure. Service industries attract economic migrants and asylum seekers, because of low pay. Bus provision is essential. Residential sprawl creates social problems. Traffic congestion is considerable. To help relieve it, Stagecoach operate the city's attractive

Passengers clambering off at one of Peterborough's Park 'n' Ride facilities, December 2002. The bus and company transit carry the Stagecoach UCOC logo. (Robert Cook)

Photographed in Bridge Street, Cambridge, August 2003, a 1996 Leyland Olympian, Cambus 573, shows the disadvantage of Transigns – when they fail they are completely illegible, hence the paper sticker in the windscreen. The bus is being operated on Stagecoach's Park 'n' Ride service. In the summer of 2004, 573 found its way to UCOC upon the arrival of smart new Dennis single-deckers. (Robert Cook)

Oxford is beyond the reach of UCOC now, but this picture, taken outside Oxford station in September 1994, shows something of the changes. A poppy red Olympian of Oxford Bus Co. is visible to the far left. In the foreground an experimental electric midi bus disgorges passengers for the railway – an image showing how hard some are working to tackle the environmental implications of so much people movement. (Robert Cook)

Park 'n' Ride. Major centres like Northampton, Peterborough, Milton Keynes and Luton are more at the centre of what is happening to Britain and all its problems, not least of which is transport.

Kitson observed in the *Milton Keynes on Sunday* on 5 September 1999, in response to outcry concerning parking charges in Milton Keynes: 'Pay Parking is unpopular and Milton Keynes Shopping Centre built part of its reputation and success on the fact that people did not have to pay. But not paying means that parking in the city centre is totally unmanageable.'

With grid-lock now affecting Milton Keynes' famous grid system, the matter of Milton Keynes' council members having access to free parking, as more of the centre's free parking spaces are converted to pay and display, angered long-time public transport campaigner Chris Wright. Responding to a *MK News* article in March 2003, he was driven to write:

Once again *MK News* has highlighted some of the very muddled thinking of our councillors. A key point of car parking was to discharge car use and force people to use the infamous buses. Thus all their concerns about access to free parking is even more scandalous. Councillors should be able to claim bus fares or perhaps a bike allowance, whichever is cheapest. The parking scheme is a muddle. Some people have not paid anything for two or three months as scratch cards did not arrive. Some were even given penalty tickets. There are several areas where signage is abysmal and unsuspecting people get tickets. Further benefits for councillors travelling by bus would be to experience delays waiting for buses, detours of MK, travel in comfort, free showers in the rain and snow, walks from the Point to the Civic Offices and thirty minutes extra travel time. If the bus is good enough for the electorate, it is good enough for councillors.

Northampton is the historic base of United Counties and in the spring of 2000 youthful contempt for its public transport system was displayed by a massive attack on the First Bus Depot. Over forty buses were put off the road, with broken windows and slashed tyres, in an early morning raid, throwing the town's services into chaos. Emergency replacement vehicles were brought in from Leicester.

Where there is a will there is a way, and the town got by, fielding a motley collection of buses for the duration of the crisis and providing a bus spotter's field day. Northampton has a long tradition of success in public transport and the arrival of Stagecoach was not without certain improvements. In December 1999, Rapid Transit Plc announced plans for a new route across south Northampton from Upton to Brackmills, via junction 15a of the M1, with Stagecoach/United Counties the preferred operator.

In September 2000 Peterborough's *Evening Telegraph* announced plans for a £100,000 computerised information system at Queensgate bus station in Peterborough. The system would include an interactive timetable to plot their journeys. It was technology designed to stop passenger confusion with old-style paper timetables. Richard Waters, the council's public transport manager said: 'The new system is very exciting. The new screens will be a breath of fresh air for our customers, as the old paper timetables are sometimes difficult to read.'

It is important not to be deluded by assumed improvements to the public transport system. Someone recently observed to one of the authors that bus travel was at one time a stately affair, with quirky bus crews imbued with a spirit of service. In the old days all sorts got on the bus and passengers were worthy of respect. So were bus crews. These days the opposite seems to be the norm. There are tales such as that reported by the *Buckinghamshire Herald* on February 24 1994: 'A furious passenger was kept on a bus against his will when he refused to pay 40p to get off early'.

The bust-up happened after John Hounslow got on the number 260 from Thame in Oxfordshire, heading for the nearby village of Haddenham. On the way home John decided to get off early as the bus passed his home in Cuddington... as he went to get off he was told he would have to pay an extra 40p... Paul Morgan, commercial manager for the Aylesbury Bus Co. – then a division of Luton and District – agreed the fare structure was absurd. There were two bus services from Thame to Haddenham; one went direct and the other via Cuddington and should cost more, but to simplify matters the fares had been made the same.

Whatever the absurdities of the fare structure, the driver, if he valued his living and the longevity of his industry, could have been more flexible. Instead he told Mr Hounslow that he would remember his face and not let him on again.

Above: A motley collection of old Leyland Nationals, photographed at Jack's Café on the A5 in summer 2003. Two serviceable buses are visible far right. They belong to Midland Routemaster, an operator seeking to do business on some of Northampton's de-regulated routes. (Robert Cook)

Right: Queensgate bus station, Peterborough, December 2002. A Stagecoach East Volvo waits on bay 16 with service 43 to Oundle. The bus station is a picture of modernity, though not so popular with older residents who think the city has lost its historic charm (Robert Cook)

By way of contrast we step back in time to Stony Stratford in the late 1960s. This bus station replaced the White House in 1963, but with the coming of Milton Keynes the site was sold for re-development. (Andrew Shouler)

Yet there is another side to the coin, as drivers themselves can face terror these days without the back-up of a conductor, as reported by the *Buckinghamshire Advertiser* on 25 November 1994:

> An Aylesbury bus driver who was terrorised by two men on a nightmare three-quarter-hour journey may leave his job. The twenty-five-year-old driver, who is too frightened to be named, has been the victim of several nasty incidents including having a knife pulled on him twice since he took up driving buses in 1991.
>
> 'At the end of the day, I just don't want to do it anymore, I want to get out of it. I want to emphasise how vulnerable bus drivers are. We have no way of communicating with anyone when we are in trouble. I have a mobile phone but I had no chance to use it'.
>
> The drama began on the Yellow Bus M11 from Motts Coaches, Stoke Mandeville, which was on a journey from Lane End to High Wycombe on Tuesday afternoon. Two men got on at Lane End and tried to pass with an invalid ticket. When the driver refused to take it they started abusing him. One of them pushed his fist in the driver's face, pinning him against the window, and as he drove off they sat next to him making comments. During the trip, they intimidated passengers, throwing one person's shopping around the single-decker.
>
> 'There were apple pies everywhere and I lingered at every stop as long as I could to pick up as many people as I could. I realised that at any moment I could get a knife in my back'

With current traffic volumes and expected growth, there can be no doubt of the need to keep trying to improve public transport. It is easier said than done as men like John Harper of Milton Keynes Council and his boss, Cabinet Member for Transport Graham Mabbutt, know only too well. Mr Mabbutt is realistic about the challenges, recognising that as long as it is so easy to get from one side of his city to another by car, then why use the bus?

Meanwhile Arriva see the potential in taking over MK Metro and we wait with interest to see whatever initiatives they might come up with. In the last analysis, however, the real initiative has to come from Central Government. Our current chancellor talks big about spending money on his pet subjects, but it is where money is spent that matters. Also it is a matter of education. On top of all that, there is this matter of anti-social behaviour, using or driving the bus at night can seem a risky business.

Driving buses at any time is quite a risk, though the professionalism of the drivers is such that passengers might hardly notice. Shortly before his retirement in the 1970s, Frank Johnson received a bronze bar for thirty-three years safe driving with United Counties. The award was presented by County Road Safety Officer E.H. Cooper. Presenting the awards after a special dinner, Mr Cooper said that accidents in the county of Northamptonshire had decreased though the number injured had increased. He said that there were 151,000 vehicles registered in the county and the number was set to double by the end of the century. He said that this made it all the more important for bus drivers to set an example to other road users. United Counties traffic manager Mr J.A. Birks pointed out that it was the Golden Jubilee year of the Road Operators Safety Council Competition. He said that last year 69,000 drivers and 35,000 conductors competed, adding: 'These people have been the foundation of the success of the United Counties Company'.

Stagecoach should certainly be congratulated for making the most of that foundation so far as United Counties is concerned. Whatever the shortcomings of their empire, they certainly evoke some of the dash and spirit of the Tilling empire that owned UCOC before nationalisation. After the Second World War, nationalisation was going to be the panacea for the nation's ills. From the Tory point of view, that approach was hamstrung by excessive bureaucracy, rigid and restrictive practices. What would have happened if Thatcher-led Tories had not won the 1979 election is anyone's guess. Would we be seeing fleets of pleasant modern and comfortable British built Leyland buses, running frequently, well-staffed, taking us to anywhere we wanted to go? Or would we have seen and under-used, heavily-subsidised old Labour dinosaurs clogging up the highways, resistant to the demands of high-density life in increasingly urbanised Britain, its employees going on strike all the time because they are underpaid, badly managed or just plain lazy and stuck in bad practices? The 1970s were notorious for industrial strife, unofficial strikes and efforts to tame the unions through legislation. Prime Minister James Callaghan, wrongly quoted as saying 'Crisis – what crisis?' – came in 1979 when his Government collapsed through a no confidence vote. The mood of the incoming Government was to destroy all solaced state dinosaurs, regardless of common sense. The bath water would go, baby and all if necessary. As for buses, how many real Tories

Above: John Harper of Milton Keynes Council, left, and Graham Mabbutt, cabinet member for transport, right. Behind them is a map of Milton Keynes grid system. As the city expands, so will their challenges and opportunities. Discouraging the private motorist from the central area has to be a priority if we are to get the best out of buses. (Robert Cook)

Above: United Counties Safe Driving awards dinner, Northampton late 1960s. (Dawn Rush)

Opposite below: An MK Metro Optare double-decker in December 2001. Travelling by bus at night, these days, can seem intimidating. (Robert Cook)

used them anyway? No member of Government was going to look seriously at traffic management problems, but asset stripping and funding tax cuts for the better off was an altogether better idea.

Maybe what happened was inevitable and there is logic to it after all. As far as Stagecoach goes, they did a lot to keep the charm going with their effective use of second-hand Routemasters, adding their exciting modern livery to all their vehicles. Moving out of Bedford/ Houghton Road, their headquarters is located in cheaper and more cost-effective premises on an industrial estate in Rosthershorpe Road – Derngate went years ago.

For the enthusiast, the use of vintage buses has been a delight. The Souters tested the strengths of Routemasters originally in their native Scotland. Recognising what a bargain they were when London Transport foolishly and slavishly started dumping them for a song – many going to Bracknell's scrapyard, they snapped them up. The buses were introduced in Bedford on service 101, across town from 1 February. On the first day of operations the service was heavily subscribed by enthusiasts but Routemasters were no miracle cure for declining bus usage in many areas.

Dealers were now moving more into the picture. All sorts of operators needed double-deckers in a hurry and body builders were very busy. Some customers specified

Taken at Northampton Dengate depot at 8 a.m. on Monday 1 May 1973, recording the result of a strike against Tory Government transport policy. Pickets guarded the entrance while a selection of Lodekkas stood idle in the side yard. There was little activity that morning, but 50 per cent of services were restored by the evening. (Andrew Shouler)

longer buses; with Stagecoach ordering extra long three-axle Olympian/Alexanders. Optare announced a decision to build a new double-deck body and Renault were moving into the British big bus market, following success in the midi bus market. There was also still a market for higher floor single-deck buses of the Duple or Plaxton-bodied Leyland Tiger variety.

Gavin Booth considered that Volvo's Mark III version of the B10M, with new 262hp or 340hp engines and easy Volvo gear shift was the most significant coaching news of the moment. The B10M was to be a part of National Express plans for their Express Liner, a standard forty-six-seat Plaxton-bodied vehicle that National Express contractors could buy or lease. The plan was to get a grip on the network which had seen some unsuitable vehicles after the disappearance of the National Bus Co.'s guiding hand. With order books filling and waiting lists growing, Gavin Booth hoped there would not be a return to the complacency of the 1970s. He thought there was hope, with manufacturers actively seeking new operators because there are no safe markets.

Those of us who remember the well ordered world of either red or green buses rolling over much of the landscape can easily forget that that particular order originated in the sometimes chaotic and cut-throat world of free market competition and pirate bus companies. The western world is highly competitive and the east is catching on fast since the Berlin Wall came down. With the US always setting the pace, there is no telling

Money makes the world go round and workers have to pay the bills. Change comes whether the little people like it or not. Among the changes to the 1970s UCOC bus scene was the demise of Derngate and the rise of Greyfriars – which opened the next day. This picture shows the last bus out of Derngate on Saturday 1 May 1976. It is the 23.05 circular to New Duston and is VRT No817, registration SRP817N. The vehicle was new in September 1974. (*Northampton Chronicle & Echo*)

United Counties depot, Rothersthorpe Road, Northampton, July 2000. The United Counties name lives on. (Robert Cook)

Greyfriars new bus station, open day May 1976. The occasion was celebrated with a gathering of enthusiasts and their vehicles. Seen here is 428, a 1952 Bristol LWL6B in DP livery, seating thirty-three and at that time owned by Rushed Enthusiasts Club. (Andrew Shouler)

On a sunny Saturday, 8 May 1971, number 159 leaves Derngate bus station on the long but picturesque route to Daventry via the Bramptons, Ravensthorpe and Long Buckby. Two fashion-conscious young ladies wait for their mates outside the café entrance. (Andrew Shouler)

An aerial view of Bedford bus station. Photographed from the adjacent multi-storey car park one Saturday in March 1972. A multitude of multiplicity is on display, including three ex-Birch saloons amongst the Lodekkas. (Andrew Shouler)

Oblivious to the danger, a young mother and her children exit the bus station in 1972 accompanied by VRT759 on service 313 and an FS Lodekka on the 256 to Weldon via Corby. The safe pathway was behind the barrier. (Andrew Shouler)

Back in August 1983 this was a bargain offer, £5 return Nottingham–London posted on the boot lid of this Leopard Supreme, number 232. The coach was one of five new in January 1979, to Luton depot – transferred to Northampton in 1983 and then to a dealer in September 1990. (Andrew Shouler)

Volvo B10M stops for passengers near Tesco in Buckingham. The vehicle is 155 with Plaxton Premiere bodywork, seating fifty-one and new in July 1993. When photographed it was allocated to Bedford but soon passed to Northampton for the slightly less strenuous X7 and X2. (Robert Cook)

An Rell6G with fifty-three-seat bus body, new in 1968, outside Luton International Airport – Luton's Corporation has taken great civic pride in the success of its airport, a pace immortalised by the Lorraine Chase Campari advert, which was so symbolic of working-class liberation. The bus looks grubby and bears the national bus insignia c.1979. This bus passed to Luton and District, when it was repainted bright red. (R.H.G. Simpson)

what new nightmares the wild west rush for development will lead to. New York alone uses more oil in a day than the whole of Africa does in a year. The United States uses more natural resources in one year than the rest of the world put together, even though only 6 per cent of the world's population live there. It is to this fast-moving world that Britain and everything within, including buses, has to adjust. Energy is a big issue and the population, particularly in the old UCOC area, is growing apace. Getting to the airport for that package holiday or European business is another aspect of modern lifestyle and Luton Airport looks set to handle even more flights.

There is a liberal view that everyone in the world has the same rights to everything. This attitude seems to be epitomised by the modern motorist who can be an irritable and often dangerous person. The sight of an empty bus lane can be a red rag to a bull for a busy motorist stuck in an expensive motor car adjacent to a bus lane. But such initiatives are vital to the future. So poor is the return on some routes that it is difficult to get anyone to tender. This seems a strange way to underpin transport in the world's fifth largest economy. Resources are concentrated on trunk routes.

The main trunk routes are operated with new modern low floor single-deckers, with specially constructed bus stops for easy access by children, mothers with baby buggies and the elderly. Service number 5 is a good example. A distinctive orange liveried Scania plies the route between Lakes Estate, Bletchley, Central Milton Keynes and north to Stony Stratford and Wolverton. Once upon a time this would have been a matter of linking little villages, but the difficulty is how to connect people living on the labyrinthine housing estates that fill the former fields along the way. Smaller Mercedes and Optare buses are one answer, but it is a complicated operation.

One interesting development is that MK Metro are now running several services both in Northampton and the southern areas of the county, under contract to the county council. They have opened a depot at Billing, to the east of town and their attractive yellow and blue livery mingles with those of standard Stagecoach and First Northampton. Their smaller midi vehicles are very suitable for the rural lanes of south Northants.

Some routes were less adaptable to Arriva's operations, and there have been other new names on the local scene. One such operated under the name 'In Motion'. It takes a bit of doing to stay in motion on the A5 through Dunstable, and the bus lane. Their manager Dave Shelley, formerly a manager for Arriva and its predecessors, told us a few years ago:

We believe that there is a niche for mid table operators offering good quality in more marginal areas. National groups flourish in the big cities, at high cost. We believe that we can make reasonable money in the areas that they neglect. For example, the Caddington–Dunstable route passes through a number of villages but was dropped because it wasn't considered viable. We have taken it on and seen a 33% growth in 12 months. Our aim is to provide a friendly, reliable service at a fair price. That doesn't mean cheap, but takes account of what it costs to drive and park. Lots of operators, like our partner company, Center Bus, in Leicester, are recognising that there is a niche market for firms like ours. We

Another Stagecoach/United Counties VolvoB10M, registration 6253 VC. This one is on the M1 motorway express service to Luton and Luton Airport from Central Milton Keynes railway station in September 2004. (Robert Cook)

Passengers alight from Easy Route 5, Optare number 7 in the MK Metro fleet, May 2000, in central Bletchley, once a proud railway and industrial town but sidelined for years as a suburb of the new Milton Keynes. The bus station is windswept and dreary and bus travel is mainly for the non motorist. (Robert Cook)

The old UCOC maintenance works at Winterhill. The site, like the railway station, was not a great success, especially following deregulation. Seen here in April 2000 with MK Metro's fitter repairing their Northern Counties bodied 'decker' which had been in collision with a car somewhere out on the busy Milton Keynes roads. The vehicle was new to Greater Manchester Transport and came via Black Prince Transport Services at Leeds. (Robert Cook)

have won contracts from Milton Keynes and Bucks County Councils, work in competition with Arriva on the X31 route and operate 18 vehicles out of two depots; Soulbury and Dunstable.

The business was absorbed into the MK Metro operation. Growing from its Milton Keynes base, MK Metro have continued their thoughtful expansion and re-routing of services, with some funded by the local council. Bucks have also helped fund the County and Silver Rider services, plugging a gap and promoting bus use. Arriva and Stagecoach have also been innovative in discount payment bus travel ideas.

At one time Arriva ran some MK local services, cutting back to the long established X15 Aylesbury to Milton Keynes and the X66 Dunstable to Milton Keynes link. The latter has recently been cut back to Dunstable from Luton town centre and airport because of the horrendous traffic congestion along the Luton to Dunstable corridor. Now most passengers for Luton and the airport use the fast Virgin train liveried service which is actually operated by Stagecoach – these coaches carry the UCOC legal lettering, running non stop via the M1.

At the time of writing MK Metro have taken over by Arriva for £5.6 million, but there are no plans to change the bright livery. MK Metro have been the most successful operator of most of the Milton Keynes services, making in-roads into Northampton. For many years they operated from the old UCOC base at Winterhill. All 260 employees are to be retained by the new owner, along with the 120 buses. Last year the MK Metro turned over £8.6 million. Arriva Commercial director Brian Drury was reported as saying that the deal was good because Milton Keynes is set to expand over the next five years, giving strong growth prospects. Arriva operates 1,400 buses in twenty-four towns outside London. The take-over brings a third major group on to the Northampton scene.

Meanwhile Stagecoach has been re-thinking their local routes. In some instances, with local authority support, they give reasonable service intervals to the towns and villages. At hourly X42 service connects Daventry via the main A45 road. This is matched by an hourly 42 service through the adjacent villages. The good people of Towcester have a half-hourly service to and from Northampton, operated by Optare Solo low floor vehicles. The number 88 service continues on westward to Brackley and the 89 south to Milton Keynes.

Northampton town services have been re-scheduled, competition with First Northampton having ceased. Each company, the latter being heir to Northampton Corporation services and fleet, now divides operations into geographical sectors. For example, East Hunsbury and the south-east village suburbs of Wootton and Hardingstone are served by Stagecoach. West Hunsbury and Briar Hill are served by First Northampton.

The long established routes across Northampton – dating back to new town development days of the early 1970s – to the Weston Favell/Duston areas have been split into radial routes 9/9A Town Centre/Duston and 1/1A Town Centre/Eastern area. This reform is an effort to overcome the awful central area traffic congestion. The cross-town routes of First Northampton have been similarly treated with Kingsthorpe, east Northampton, Far Cotton and St James services not proceeding beyond the central bus station. Stagecoach vehicles use particularly clear and effective diagrammatic route maps on the side window nearest the entrance door so intending passengers can browse as they wait to board. Both companies use dedicated low floor access vehicles. Stagecoach have retained a monopoly of local services in the UCOC old stomping ground in Wellingborough, Kettering, Corby, and Bedford – the latter seems to get most of the new vehicles.

Bus operators and would-be bus operators know there is a going to be a much bigger market for their services and their time will come. Milton Keynes was designed for motor cars, but the council is discouraging car use through extending parking charges and opening more bus lanes. We've heard the slogan let the train take the strain, now it must be time for 'let the bus take the fuss'!

Much more needs to be done, however, if buses are going to get people out of cars in sufficient numbers to ease environmental harm. There are a lot of initiatives to get more people on to the buses. In Northampton, all three operators issue their own day

This Rell6G, just arrived at Cambridge Drummer Street in the mid-1970s, is a world away from the buses of the modern varsity city. Number 306 in Biggleswade's allocation; it was one of eight new in October 1967, withdrawn in the early 1980s. (R.H.G. Simpson)

Drummer Street on a sunny Sunday in July 2003 shows evidence of a facelift and a rather different sort of bus. This long wheel base, but un identified Olympian/Alexander is in Stagecoach service in what used to be the furthest eastern reach of UCOC buses. (Robert Cook)

rider tickets, valid only on the route for which they are purchased. The Northampton Buzz Card is an innovative scheme, launched in January 2006, in conjunction with Northamptonshire County Council and the bus companies. Costing £3 per day or £11 a week, it gives the user unlimited travel within the town area. Considering it costs £1.30 for a single journey from Duston to Greyfriars, it is a bargain. So is the Stagecoach Dayrider at £2.30. Safer, cleaner and more comfortable bus stations and stops would help as travelling long distance and after dark can be dangerous.

Winterhill Bus Depot in Milton Keynes has been sold and the bus station hardly used. Fourteen years ago a *Buses Magazine* article by Tim Carter suggested that Milton Keynes 'has been finished with good transport connections to the outside world'. The report argued that many coach services, for the sake of convenience and drivers' hours, did not stray off the M1 to drive into Milton Keynes central bus station. Matters were resolved when a new coach stop was provided at an information point about 100m from Junction 14 of the M1 and National Express's timetable was amended accordingly.

The council were hopeful that the new Coachway would increase the number of passengers joining coaches thirty fold. The Coachway was linked to the city centre by a minibus shuttle service. One effect of this innovation was to make the marble-clad central bus station even less relevant. The Milton Keynes on Sunday newspaper announced, in February 2000, that the city's bus station and depot was to be sold to solve the council's cash crisis caused by overspending.

It has not been all bad news in the old UCOC area. The company's heirs, Stagecoach, introduced an excellent series of express services under the brand name of 'Inter County' in at the turn of the twentieth/twenty-first century. Their regularity, reliability, comfort and speed were well appreciated by passengers.

Some of these services have the backing of Central and Local Government, but the X5 from Oxford to Cambridge, via Milton Keynes, Bedford and St Neots is a commercial service. The service is so popular that it runs every thirty minutes, seven days a week. Duties are carried out by the Bedford depot and the first Sunday coach leaves town, heading west to Oxford, where it arrives at 7.35 a.m., before returning east to Cambridge at 7.45 a.m. The corresponding first service to Cambridge leaves Bedford at 6.40 a.m.

The X4 service operates from Milton Keynes to Peterborough, via Northampton, Wellingborough, Kettering, Corby and Oundle. It is operated by Kettering depot with a half-hourly service between Milton Keynes and Corby and hourly extensions to Peterborough. From the Northampton depot, the X7 connects Northampton and Leicester, the X2 Northampton to Bedford, and the X6 Northampton to Oxford. The drivers play a crucial role in promoting these services and are most helpful. The X4 has the added joy, for us males, of the feminine touch, with several pleasant ladies behind the wheel.

Such people are very different from the rugged and robust hands on individuals who pioneered the Wellingborough Omnibus Co. and all the other transport concerns. Managers usually come from college, having attended training schemes, and technical staff from shortened courses to allow for skills shortage. Bus drivers are in short supply

One of MK Metro's Mercedes Vario Plaxton Beaver 2s, passes All Saints Church, heading for the Drapery in the summer of 2003. It will wait there for passengers for its return to Milton Keynes, via Newport Pagnell. The advert on the bus's side indicates continuing efforts to recruit drivers. (Robert Cook)

because the job is highly stressful, underpaid, dangerous and lonely compared to the old days when they worked in crews.

Finding staff to operate the buses can be difficult because the cost of living in Milton Keynes is so high. With an income of £35,000 necessary to buy the most basic house, people are moving north of where they work, increasingly commuting. Lots of council houses have fallen into the private rented sector and more affluent London and commuting over spill also pushes up prices and influences the pattern of demand for public transport. Good public transport requires a change in consumer attitudes and enormous and sustained public investment. Tram systems seem to have style appeal, but as former rail boss Sir Bob Reid said, they only suit particular environments and are not the answer for Milton Keynes, but what is? What are the answers for those less well-off or incapable of driving cars, and living in the rural outposts of the old UCOC area? It is easier to ask questions that provide answers. Certainly we cannot expect much from Government just now. With so much expansion happening in the South East, the £51 million for transport infrastructure to go with it, just offered by the ODPM (Office of the Deputy Prime Minister) is a pittance, though rail operators are doing very nicely nationwide. The rail network receives almost £5 billion from the public purse even

An unidentified MK Metro Mercedes Vario/Plaxton Beaver 2, new in 1999, exits from gloomy Greyfriars bus station in February 2006, working service 87 to Towcester via numerous country lanes villages under contract to Northamptonshire County Council. (Andrew Shouler)

Bathed in winter sunshine, Stagecoach's Volvo/Alexander waits to work service 33 to Northampton via the villages. New in 1997 to Stagecoach Manchester, it was recently exchanged for a similarly aged Olympian/Northern Counties decker, which passed to UCOC from Cambus. (Andrew Shouler)

Stagecoach Olympian/Alexander 18109, registration KX04RV, waits to take the half-hourly X4 service from outside Milton Keynes Theatre, to Peterborough in January 2006. (Robert Cook)

Bus stop view, Central Milton Keynes, almost from the driving seat of UCOC Alexander-bodied Leopard in August 1982. The bus in front is MK allocation UCOC 924, a VRT Series 3, new in April 1980, working the 410 local service. The bus passed to Milton Keynes City Bus in January 1986. (Andrew Shouler)

Nottingham used to be on the UCOC express list of destinations. Today it is as congested as the average British city and has found a part answer through a modern tram system. Trams look continental and cool. Buses, once the liberators of the masses, are perceived as common. (Nicola Cook)

though there has been little improvement to services since 1997. The price of standard long-distance tickets has increased 10.2 per cent – around four times the rate of inflation. Eighty per cent of the Government's transport budget is spent on the railways, according to their own figures. Sir Bob Reid, last chairman of British Rail, informed Robert Cook that he had told Government that privatisation was not a good idea and if they had to do it, his board had a better model. They did not listen. So much for privatisation. This is a very different world for the Stagecoach remnant of UCOC, though of course their parent company benefits from rail franchising.

7

No Return

There can be no return to an idyllic age of bus travel. The Golden Age, if there is one, has to be now. Life moves on. If you try standing still, you perish. The question is, where does one move on to in life? As this story has told, in the early days of busmanship, many roads were little more than cart tracks. Real improvements to the trunk road network began in the 1930s, but they never kept pace with the expansion of road haulage, bus and coach travel, let alone the ineffable rise of the private motorist. Motorways began in the late 1950s, with the opening of the first section of the M1 doing much to speed up coach travel, and other motorways and improvements followed slowly.

Meanwhile, bus travel outside the capital and other major British cities, began steadily to decline. New bus stations were opened, taking advantage of cheap concrete construction, and they always managed to look cheap and in stark contrast to the artistic merits of early Tilling structures, as found around the UCOC area. The main objective for new bus stations was efficiency. Aylesbury's teeming Kingsbury Square gave way for the underground world of Friars Square in 1968. Luton and Northampton were similarly blessed. These functional, unimaginative designs and often threatening environments are hardly advertisements for the virtues and modernity of bus transportation. Folk have a much greater, if not misplaced, sense of security inside their motor cars. They also, usually, seem to think they look better.

Whilst investment in public transport has been inadequate and the private funding no panacea, life for the motorist has not been made easier and some think this is deliberately so. If life on the road gets bad enough, some cynics suspect, folk will have to use buses and so buses become more viable. Change came quickly in the wake of de-regulation, though a lot of old buses were kept in service. Even Milton Keynes bus station has lingered on.

You can not run a decent transport system of any sort without investing in good roads. In Britain this is an afterthought. Nationally the road maintenance bill has risen by 12 per cent because repairs went undone. The maintenance bill now stands at £8.4 billion – so much for Government plans! Inevitably John Dawson of the AA saw road building and improvements like widening the M1 between the M25 and M1 in Milton Keynes, as the solution. Without it, business and sacred economic growth would suffer. Meanwhile

Aylesbury, Friars Square bus station in May 2000. It is gloomy, dirty, noisy and smelly. In spite of a facelift, the waiting room is drab and cramped. Litter and spilled liquid creates an unpleasant collage around the bus bays. (Robert Cook)

MK Metro Bus and car share road space in central Milton Keynes, February 1999. The city goes on growing, along with the traffic. The solitary bus passenger looks stolidly ahead in stark contrast to the smiling car people, full of the joys of the open road in their sporty cabriolet, top down in spite of winter. How can there be a modal shift when the contrasts are as this image suggests? (Robert Cook)

Central Milton Keynes bus station, November 2002, still sees a little traffic but it was an idealistic failure for 1970s planners. Extra coaches, belonging to 'On a Mission' were employed on rail replacement services during the West Coast Main Line upgrading work. (Robert Cook)

Friends of the Earth feared more roads would encourage more driving and important natural sites would disappear under tarmac.

Lack of foresight and a national obsession with cars has impacted badly in these places. Authorities are facing up to the problem but progress is slow. Initiatives like those of Buckinghamshire County Council's Stefan Dominic may seem silly, but he makes an interesting point when saying that leaving your car at home for one day a week means a reduction in traffic of 20 per cent. His scheme to encourage walking and cycling policies has won awards. Buckinghamshire cannot even afford to improve its roads into the expanding Milton Keynes and such bus services that have replaced the old United Counties efforts provide no slack or underpinning in times of overload. There is also the reality of too frequently changing operators and running a sparse timetable. Good public transport requires considerable fair subsidy, in line with what it is worth paying to protect the quality of lives and environment.

Northamptonshire County Council produced a 'Local Transport Plan 2001–2006', that tied in with the Government's ten-year transport plan, including £3 million on road improvements. These days £3 million is not much and there is little reference to public transport. It really adds up to make do and mend as far as buses are concerned because at the moment it is a poor relation. Privatisation is about profit and company's like First cannot sensibly ignore the fact that it is easier to make money out of their trains than buses.

As long as traffic flounders around, as it does, and road carnage remains high, there is a case to answer and the counties are far from united – though through current

Some old buses rolled on during the de-regulation transition period. Here we see a pockmarked Leyland National, number 547, bearing Luton Bus nomenclature. It was an ex-UCOC vehicle, new in 1978 and passed to Luton & District in January 1986. Its companion, in the old Aylesbury UCOC backyard, is VRT number 753, a VRT whose original flat front was upgraded to series 3 specification – curved screen etc., in May 1982. It too passed to Luton 7 District in 1986. (R.H.G. Simpson)

Government policies toward total control of everything, our historic counties may soon be a thing of the past in any case.

Meanwhile public transport is a world of opportunities for companies with initiative. The danger is that corporate goals displace the primary objective of moving people about as conveniently and cheaply as possible. To this end peoples' needs must be recognised as they were in the days of the old stage wagons and carriers carts, when needs were met according to technology available. Companies like Arriva, whose routes extend south beyond the old United Counties ones, knew this when they set up the 325 bus around Princess Risborough, linking town, housing estates and shops in February 1999. Commercial Director Nigel Eggleton said at the time 'New route 325 provides a useful link for Princess Risborough. To encourage as many people as possible to give it a try, Arriva is more than happy to mail the timetable leaflet free of charge'.

Since 1979, through the Government's battle for the free market in almost everything, we have paid the price through growing car ownership, more and more joy riding and trips to out of town shopping centres. Car drivers have a spurious sense of freedom and often a sense of importance related to the size, age and model of the car they drive. Many will boast that their vehicles are environmentally friendly – a ludicrous boast. Most car journeys are under 3 miles, too little for catalytic converters to be effective and lead-free petrol and diesel just emit different sorts of poison. Life on the buses as crew or passenger was a different world and now it is a lost one.

Lodekkas lingered on in Thatcher's Brave New World of free enterprise. These FSB Lodekkas were withdrawn in March 1981 and are seen here in the last days at Houghton Road, having been converted to buttercup yellow as a warning to other unsuspecting road users that they were being used for driver training. All of them were new back in 1966 when England swung like 'a pendulum do'. Originally 714–718, they were renumbered 1005–1109. A Leopard/Dominant II stands new and as yet to be allocated, on the right. It is registration VNH169W. (Andrew Shouler)

National Express survived de-regulation through a management buy-out and can boast offering the largest scheduled coach service provision in Europe, travelling to 1,000 destinations and carrying 16 million customers a year, a lot of them students from our proliferating universities, along with the dirty washing they are taking home to mum. The world has moved on since folk took the bus to the market town. This is the age of mass air travel and the major airports have to be served.

Getting buses to the airports seems to have become a priority to the apparently most discontented folk in Europe (according to Phillipe Auclair's book *Blair's Magical Kingdom*). To hell with getting to work, let's just get away. It is all a far cry from Bill Horwood's bus ride to work at UCOC's main works in the late 1940s. The summer of 2003 has broken records for heat waves. Network Rail imposed 60mph speed restrictions because its continuously welded rails, of lower standard than the rest of Europe, are in danger of buckling and Megabus's Oxford Tube has annoyed its competitor Oxford Bus by offering on-line fares of £1 to London. Is this a sign that the crowded South East is in the grip of anything resembling a transport strategy? Meanwhile traffic jams generated record noxious fumes, boosting ozone and smog hazards. In 2005 Buckinghamshire County Council reported a falling road and transport budget at the same time as an expanding Milton Keynes will increase demands on their highways. A long and expensive inquiry process into the expansion of Milton Keynes, Luton and Northampton has no firm plans for alternatives to cars and lorries.

Left: Former Lodekka number 715 dates from 1966 and is seen here at Stoke Mandeville after conversion by UCOC into tree lopping and general factotum for bus stop post work in 1981. It passed to Luton & District in January 1986, when it was decorated in a buttercup yellow livery complete with Luton & District bright red band. (Tom Goodwin)

Below: Photographed in August 2003 National Express at Drummer Street bus station, a busy interchange and loading point, especially for the student population. The company became a separate and private entity, leasing vehicles, following de-regulation. National Express is a strong part of the industry. (Robert Cook)

Bearing the Stagecoach United Counties fleet name in May 2000, 693 is leaving Buckingham for Northampton, Market Harborough, Leicester and the long (in miles) and lengthy (in time) via Oxford, Bicester, Buckingham, Northampton and Leicester. This bus, an Olympian/Alexander eighty-seven-seater, was new in October 1997 and is still (in 2006) busy at work in the three counties of Northants, Beds and Bucks. Fitted with bus seats, it was a feat of endurance to travel the full length of the route. There are apocryphal stories of passengers having to be helped off at the termini. At least the next year's delivery of S-registered stock (in October 1998) had dual-purpose seats. (Robert Cook)

An RAC report recently revealed that British commuters spend more time travelling to work than any others in Europe. How much easier if they all got on the bus! The average distance travelled is 8.5 miles, a 17 per cent increase on the last decade. Outside of London 72 per cent of commuters use their cars to get to work, 28 per cent use buses and 5 per cent use trains. The rest walk or cycle. Local authorities like Buckinghamshire's struggle to promote public transport, gaining concessionaire fares for their employees, In December 1994, Buckinghamshire County Council published an integrated transport strategy for the county, noting that:

> Traffic is increasing faster than roads can cope with. The days of carefree motoring are over. Everyone knows the frustration of sitting in traffic jams, not just in big cities but driving locally as well. Commuters compete for road space with mothers driving to school. A journey which used to take only five minutes by car now takes much longer.
>
> In addition, the environment is deteriorating with traffic fumes and noise. Emissions are bad for peoples' health and people are finding it less safe to walk because of speeding traffic.

Buckinghamshire County Council's Integrated Transport Strategy was intended to influence the demand for travel and the way that it was met. They aimed to reduce

Above: There is still a market for bus travel for a mass market among impoverished students, as this picture of Megabus 6 Wheel Olympian, at the University of East Anglia shows us, in February 2006. The bus is an ex-Hong Kong City Bus; used to coping with high population density demand, it returned to the UK in 2003. Great Yarmouth First EC took delivery of ten of these vehicles – presumably for high summer season. (Robert Cook)

Left: Once a western outpost of UCOC and still enjoying their services in the 1970s, this is Gloucester Green in January 2003. Curving bus lines of the Oxford Tube and curvy tubular columns of the bus stations are almost an antithesis of design, yet create a quiet harmony. (Nicola Cook)

pollution, traffic congestion and accidents. Nearly ten years later, progress has not been good. The situation has got worse, albeit at a slower rate on the pollution front due to improved engine technology.

The same is true throughout the old United Counties area as Government encourages more South East development and planning rules to slacken accordingly. Council employees may well get subsidised public transport usage, but the medium is generally seen as inconvenient and something more suited to the lower classes. Far better to show off your new car, even if it involves sitting in a traffic jam for several hours. But woe betides you if your number plate is getting dated. In 2001 *Auto Express* conducted a survey of 500 drivers. This revealed that one in ten male drivers has been physically attacked. The older the car, the greater the risk, with 13 per cent of G-registration car owners and 15 per cent of J-registration car owners having been physically assaulted.

Those forced to use buses may be seen as even lower in the pecking order and suffer equal abuse. The *Milton Keynes Herald* carried this report on 8 December 1994:

> Coach Passengers shaken by vandal. Coach passengers had a lucky escape when a brick was thrown from a city over bridge, smashing into the vehicle's windscreen. Fortunately, neither the driver nor his passengers were injured, although they were said to be shaken.
>
> This was the latest in a series of incidents and police have warned drivers to be wary of anyone walking across city over bridges.
>
> The latest act of vandalism cost coach company Soul's of Olney £1,200 to repair the damage... the coach was making its way from Denbigh where it had picked up workers to take them home... Kevin Lyne, general manager at Soul's said: 'Fortunately the screen was laminated, so it cracked, but didn't fall inwards – otherwise it could have been a lot worse...'

What kind of person would do such a thing? These crazy days there might be no telling, but in this case police were looking for a white man about 6ft tall, with a thin face, reddish hair and wearing dark clothing. But bus passengers were not necessarily being singled out – back in October of that year a paving slab was hurled at a BMW and a plastic bottle filled with concrete was thrown at a Ford Escort from Milton Keynes bridges.

Summer 2004 has shown us just how much worse matters have become. Skyscrapers at Canary Wharf were wreathed in dirty brown smog as rising temperatures, stagnant air and vehicle pollutants trapped harmful ozone at ground level across the capital and other big settlements. Logic should tell us that the car's days should be numbered or use at least taxed according to mileage. Interestingly 80 per cent of journeys are under 6 miles and catalytic converters are ineffective until vehicles have completed the first three journey miles. Milton Keynes Council faces the mother of all problems in a continuously growing settlement that was designed – if that is not too strong a word – around the motor car. It is hard to imagine an alternative solution, especially given the psychological identification that local drivers have formed with their vehicles – so much so that even if locals can't buy a car they might be inclined to join the record number of car thieves in the area – because you simply have to be seen in a cool motor if you are a self-respecting Milton Keynesian!

Buckinghamshire County Council, like other authorities, is up against the odds. In 1994 they announced twenty-year targets, including: a cut in the proportion of people using their cars to get to work from 70 per cent in 1991 to 60 per cent by 2011, an increase in the number of people getting to work by public transport, from 9 per cent in 1991 to 15 per cent by 2011 and a similar increase for those getting to work on foot. In January 2000 it published findings from a series of participation meetings leading up to the Provisional Local Transport Plan. (LTP) Chiltern residents responded to the 2000 survey by saying that they would use the car less if there was cheaper public transport, safer walking and a frequent bus service which ran on time. Further observations included that car drivers were becoming increasingly aggressive, that it was no use creating speed limits, zebra crossings, etc. or painting white lines on roads if drivers did not observe them. But what can be done about it?

Improved services would require more taxation or diverting funds from a variety of current worthy or unworthy causes. As for controlling motorists, such is the self-righteousness of some that the *Bucks Herald* recently reported on Aylesbury anti-speeding protester Paul Newman who has ' taken to standing by the road to warn fellow drivers there are police speed traps ahead, after being caught speeding in a 30mph zone'. The Southcourt resident had refused to pay a £60 speeding fine and taken to standing close to where he was caught with a sign reading '30mph speed trappers ahead'. He told the paper, 'We have lost our freedom as soon as we step outside the door we are being told what to do'.

On the same page the *Bucks Herald* reported that Princess Risborough may be turned into a one-way system to ease the crippling traffic congestion. 'Double yellow lines are failing to stop people parking illegally, thus clogging up the High Street and Market Square. Town Council Clerk, Dennis Phillips, said it would be difficult to find a solution to please everybody. Local bus company, Arriva, said a one way system would force it to change some of its routes with some services no longer stopping in the town centre. Spokesperson, Kate Flint, said "Reduced access would have a very negative effect on customers, many of whom are elderly and may have difficulty walking any distance to less central shops".'

North Buckinghamshire and South Northamptonshire experience some different problems. These days the area is rife with multiple car-owning families who can clog up the roads, while the less fortunate wait for dwindling bus services. Among North Buckinghamshire people's comments to the LTP were requests for greater frequency of bus services linking towns and large villages, more rural bus services and links to rail. Respondents to the survey also called for more low floor buses to ease entry for the less mobile who are more likely to use them. Car ownership is taken for granted in modern Britain and specialist credit companies offer car loans to bad debtors as if a car is a right. Yes Car Credit poses the question, 'Refused car credit? We'll say Yes, whatever your credit history'. Sadly, you can't ride the buses on credit!

It has been shown that city traffic nowadays moves more slowly than in the old days of horse and carts. Bus lanes anger some motorists who fail to see a need to give public

Stagecoach X2 service hurtles into Bedford, September 2005. The bus is standard Stagecoach stock, number 52371, registration P171 KBD, Volvo B10M. The authors recall when Leyland sold buses to the Swedes. Where did it all go wrong? (Robert Cook)

Ryan Beveridge at Bletchley bus station, an awful and windswept place in July 2004. He made a plea on behalf of single parents with pushchairs. There is just not enough room on the buses for pushchairs and baggage. (Robert Cook)

service vehicles priority. A spate of accidents involving coaches on motorways led to calls to ban them from outside lanes. This provoked an angry response from some operators fearing that services would appear 'slow coaches' alongside flashy modern motor cars. Tory Secretary of State Brian Mawhinney made the decision to ban coaches from outside lanes of motorways with three or more lanes, from 1 January 1996, for a trial period of two years so that accident data could be examined. Speaking to the *Buckingham & Winslow Advertiser*, Graham Smith, sales director of Heyfordian Travel, based at Upper Heyford, said he did not see the need for a ban, adding that it could slow down travel time. He explained that if you have two trucks travelling side by side the coach would have to slow down as well. Mr Smith added that the ban could result in two drivers being needed for Continental travel as their travel time would be slowed down. That could result in price increases for travellers.

Andy Price, manager of Steeple Claydon, based Langston & Tasker, who benefited from the break-up of UCOC monopoly in the Buckingham area, said the ban could result in convoys of coaches and lorries on motorways. He said his drivers try to keep the speed down anyway but if you are on the motorway you don't pootle along at 45 to 50mph – you go as fast as the conditions allow. He added: 'When you take the amount of coaches on the roads and the number of accidents, they are, as a percentage, very low'.

Nearly twenty years later Milton Keynes had not sorted out its public transport plan. The *Milton Keynes Gazette* reported on 2 May 1991 that: 'Almost two years is a pretty long time to wait for a bus… even in Milton Keynes. But waiting – and campaigning – has finally paid off for residents of Whalley Drive in Bletchley. Having lost their original bus service in August 1989, only two months after local authorities had spent out to have Whalley Drive and Sherwood Drive fitted with brand new bus shelters. Mrs Chris Simpson, secretary of the Bletchley Park Residents Association, told the *Milton Keynes Gazette*: 'We've been campaigning for the service to be reinstated ever since then, helped by Cllr Gillingham'.

It took them until April 1991 to get the buses back in their locality, the first bus arriving at 9.15 a.m., bang on time. Chris Simpson, was among the first aboard. She commented: 'It has been worth it. We weren't simply campaigning for ourselves. It was for everyone who uses Whalley Drive, Sherwood drive, the Community Hospital and The Coppice. There wasn't even a stop outside the rail station; the nearest stop was in Buckingham Road', said Chris.

The first buses had been a novelty, but soon became transport for the masses, cheek by jowl, jam-packed together. The best sign that a route was worth running was the number of folk on board, seated and standing. Nowadays folk want a bit more privacy in a society that is watching them more than ever. Jam-packed together like sardines on the buses, where people shout and holler, cough, sneeze and even commit anti-social acts, it's not surprising people avoid them. Terrorism has been further discouragement to using public transport, unless absolutely unavoidable.

Stagecoach, for all its early success has found the going increasingly tough. Expansion into the US has not been as rewarding as expected, partly because buses have lost their cool over there too. In an attempt to revive his group's ailing share price, in March 2000, Brian Souter was reported to be taking a knife to the empire. A sale of the £1.3 billion Porterbrook train-leasing arm to banker Abbey National was said to be imminent.

The business, which owned about a third of Britain's trains, was forecast to make 40 per cent of the bus and train group's profits that year. A sale would provide cash to expand further into the US and Far East and bouncing share prices could pave the way to a New York listing. All this high finance is worlds away from pre-de-regulation days and was it really what the Tories intended when they spoke of getting rid of public-owned public transport monoliths – or was the only objective an ideological war on state enterprise?

What else could they do? It is difficult to improve a situation controlled by vested interests. Plans for a new public transport route across the south of Northampton have already been mentioned and were reported by the *Northampton Chronicle & Echo* on 9 December 1999. Rapid Transit International Plc were planning a route from Upton in the west to Brackmills, travelling via junction 15a of the M1 and Wootton. The route, the report said, could be built by 2002. Alex Carter, managing director of Stagecoach – United Counties, RTI's preferred operator said:

> Line six is a key piece in the jigsaw of rapid transit for our town.
>
> An efficient clean and modern public transport system for Northampton is getting closer and this corridor will ensure thousands more individuals and families will have the opportunity to use a transport system for the new millennium. New stations and new sections of guided tramways will be built as part of the Line six outline plans which have been submitted to the borough council.
>
> Stations are planned in Upton, Pineham, Swan Valley, junction 15a of the M1, Milton Ham, Hunsbury station, Hunsbury West, Wooton, Hardingstone and Brackmills.

The report added that the location of new stations had not yet been decided, but RTI development director Mike Kendrick said they should be where the maximum number of passengers would use them. He said, 'We are trying to put in as much new infrastructure as possible, but sometimes it is too expensive or impractical and we have to use existing infrastructure'. He said most of the guided tracks and new stations would be built in new developments which were still in the planning stages. Not surprisingly there is little evidence of Line Six at time of writing this – May 2006. It would seem that there is little chance of it being revived.

On August bank holiday 2003 the *Mail on Sunday* reported that it became a bank holiday to remember with 20-mile traffic jams. Of course the Government is thinking and talking about solutions, like 'road user charging'. In July 2003, former Transport Supremo, Socialist and Jaguar fan John Prescott, told the *Daily Mirror*: 'I coined the phrase "You can't build your way out of congestion" and what I believed then and believe now was that I don't think you can solve it by building new roads.' What can he possibly mean? Does he secretly like buses and trains or does he want people to stay home. Minister Alistair Darling talked of a £7 billion roads package while a new survey by the Institution of Civil Engineers says that 75 per cent of roads are cracking up and £7.4 billion of repairs were needed in 2002.

It is hard to imagine how corporation transport in towns the size of Northampton might have developed without de-regulation. Monopolies legislation prevented Stagecoach taking over all United Counties and Corporation business in 1985, as had happened when United Counties took over from Luton Corporation many years earlier. First Bus became the eventual long-term successors to Northampton Borough Transport and now the council is only involved in terms of inviting tenders for routes. This might have seemed like an opportunity for entrepreneurs in 1985, like the brief appearance of Midland Routemaster, operating on Northampton routes 11, 13, 14 and 54 and based at Jack's Hill Cafe, on the A5 west of Towcester.

Life in the bus lane is not that easy. Nowadays the council's major function is route subsidy. The borough currently spends £144,000 a year and has an on top agreement with the county council, all county contracts going through the borough at a charge of £175,000. Measured in terms of the size of the growing town, it may not seem very much. The tendering procedure, according to the 1985 Transport Act, allows five years operation. A problem with privatisation is that if there is not enough profit or subsidy, no one will tender. At the time of writing, a council spokesman said, 'We have a commercial network of routes and commercial network of services'. Stagecoach United Counties are covering the ex-Midland Routemaster routes on an hourly basis. With their greater resources they are in a position to take a longer view and encourage more bus use.

Optimism and rural bus services are almost contradictions in terms. In April 1994 the *Buckingham Advertiser* newspaper announced that public transport was given a boost with the launch of improved coach services for Buckingham, Brackley and Bicester. Free rides were being offered on a new weekday service from Oxford to Bicester and Buckingham. United Counties and Coachlinks promised speedier journeys and extra services linking the three towns with Oxford in response to public demand. Because the number of passengers between Bicester and Oxford had been increasing, fares have not had to rise for nearly two years. Rod Davies, Coachlinks' Oxfordshire manager said his company had been listening to existing and potential customers.

Extra journeys were operated between Oxford and Buckingham and a new weekly service would leave Oxford at 5.10 p.m. for Bicester and Buckingham. No fares would be charged for a week. Another coach would leave Oxford for Bicester at 5.40 p.m., with limited stops to get passengers home earlier. Some services would also go through to Leicester, and Nottingham but locals would be welcome to use them, said Mr Davies. A weekly fare from Oxford to Bicester was just the ticket at £9 for adults and £5 for children and students.

There had been hope that after years of Tory ideological devastation of public transport that the New Labour Government, elected in 1997, would get down to dealing with transport matters more effectively. Time revealed that there was a more abstract agenda of social engineering and spin doctoring above all else. This should not have come as a surprise because Labour never quite managed to get near their 1945 promise of an integrated transport system – that would have taken far too much political courage!

First Bus services on Briar Hill Estate, Northampton, February 1996. It was then a tough estate and probably still is. Buses are a life line for many. (Robert Cook)

A Volvo B6, with Wright Crusader loads up in Upper George Street, central Luton, in January 2002. It was one of eleven to UCOC's successor in January 2002. (Robert Cook)

But in early days there was a little optimism when Transport Minister Gavin Strang announced cash that would improve services in the Buckingham and Winslow area among others. Not surprisingly there never was any serious money, just a measly £41.7 million programme to improve rural services across Britain.

Buckinghamshire was told that its investment allocation would be £570,000, Northamptonshire would get £690,000 and Oxfordshire £930,000. Every little helps of course, but over the years since, there have been continuing threats to services and overall they are of questionable standard and reliability because there is not just the money in it and if you provide a rough service it can be no surprise if you only get rough trade. Tingewick residents on the Oxfordshire and Buckinghamshire County borders had to fight a hard campaign to restore their Saturday bus service to Buckingham, announcing their victory in January 2003. They faced the prospect of being left stranded when, in November 2002, bus operator Jeffs announced it was cutting the service for being uneconomical.

Privatisation may have been offered up as hope for better bus services, but with the demise of UCOC, new operators would be constrained by harsher economic realities and the rural community would suffer. Rosemary Stuchbury launched a campaign to save her local route which also covered Gawcott, raising 250 names on a petition and sending letters to PM Tony Blair, MP John Bercow and county councillors. Many campaigners relied on the bus to take them to shops or work and their lobbying paid off when another operator, Easy Bus said it would run the Saturday service from Finmere and Tingewick. They announced that there would be four buses to Buckingham on Saturday plus a service to Banbury – a route originally covered by Midland Red – but there would be no direct bus to Milton Keynes. Mrs Stuchberry was jubilant, saying that her family didn't have a car and never did have, but relied on shopping in Buckingham at weekends. She thanked the county council's senior transport officer for helping to get the service restored.

Facts must be faced, people prefer cars. Those by dint of income, age, principle or disabilty, do not have the freedom of the days before de-regulation. As to the way life used to be with United Counties before de-regulation, there is just no return for the foreseeable future. Councils look at various ideas. In recent years we have heard of initiatives like the one for Olney where in 1997, councillors were trying to provide a minibus but have been put off by huge costs of £50,000 a year to lease, staff and run the bus. They had wanted it to provide a bus to transport elderly people to day care facilities in town as well as making it available for local sports clubs and other organisations. 'The costs were frightening', said Cllr Brian Partridge after visiting two day care centres at St Giles in Stony Stratford and Netherfield, Milton Keynes to inspect a minibus. He explained: 'It became clear how expensive an issue transportation is. The costs were high because three members of staff were needed, including a driver, assistant and a back up member of staff.'

Further south in the old UCOC area, the following year, Winslow were given a £100,000 to buy a community minibus. Buckinghamshire County Council were handed cash by the Government to introduce the service in the new year. It will be available

Arriva the Shires and Essex 5157 Volvo Olympian/Northern Counties Palatine stops outside Cantell's Stores, May 2000, in Winslow High Street on its journey back from Buckingham and on its way to Aylesbury. Luton and District's successor, this bus was one of fifteen new in 1998 and carries a Hertforshire registration. (Robert Cook)

A lot of the old UCOC Tilling assets made good money following de-regulation and re-development for expensive town centre housing. This is old UCOC Aylesbury UCOC garage in Buckingham Road, in May 1999, almost gone, demolished to make way for desirable homes enabling more people to commute to the metropolis. A hint of the old Tilling majesty in bus station and depot design is just discernible. (Robert Cook)

for use by the public and a variety of groups, charities and organisations which operate from the town and surrounding villages. 'The minibus was intended for two basic roles. One was for a conventional bus service links between Winslow, surrounding villages and maybe Buckingham at times when there is no other public transport available. The other purpose was for hiring out to local groups. John Hodgkins, Buckinghamshire County Council Transport Officer described the innovation as excellent news. The bus was intended to serve Whaddon, Nash, Thornbrough, the Horwoods, Claydons, Swanbourne, Mursley and Granborough. Winslow also had the benefit of a sparse bus service to Milton Keynes and a continuation of the old UCOC service 346 through the good offices of Arriva.

All these little buses running around in a sea of motor cars and lumbering juggernauts just is not the same as in the good old days. A lot of them do not even look like the real buses we remember and one wonders how folk will look back upon these tumultuous times. Will today's young provide the same number of bus spotters, nostalgic retired employees and enthusiasts? Will there be anything to be nostalgic about?

8

Missing Buses

A wise old man from Bedford once said the golden age is now. There is no return ticket to the past, except in our minds. When we listen to stories from the past, he said, 'People will only tell you about the battles we won'. Of course history is selective and there is a great deal of opinion expressed in these closing chapters.

History is full of epochs, new worlds beckoning and disappointments. Horse buses were a nineteenth-century invention and Thomas Tilling was our greatest pioneer. Motor buses were a twentieth-century phenomenon with their heyday in the 1930s. Post-Second World War, the Socialist dreams of perfect infrastructure, transport included, never quite got off the ground, but the 1960s were still the age of the motor bus for most people. Then came the showdown with the unions and free enterprise was all the rage.

So superficially, at least, we can look back on quieter times when Tilling green and poppy red added to the rambling charm of post-war Britain. The buses may not have always been on time, but that was part of the fun, so was chasing the ones that came early or wondering when the late one would arrive – and sometimes it did not. Buses were sociable moving communities. On the rural, and even town, routes, of UCOC, those communities were never so large that individual identities were lost. Youth rode them to the pictures and the back seat on the way home was the place for a bit of slap and tickle. Many workers rode the same route for years, always talking of the same mutual acquaintances and of subjects like sport, the weather, who was having an affair with who, who was having a baby and who had died. Young men might rush to follow a mini-skirted beauty onto the top deck and wayward youth would be put off early to walk home on roads a lot safer than they are today. And so, in this final chapter, we look at a few more images of the buses we miss, from the years we miss.

Though United Counties has its history of Leylands and Bristols, it has used a number of odds and ends. Fred Newman referred disparagingly to the company's Willowbrook Fords as 'Fish n' Chip Vans'. Obviously it would be impossible to preserve examples of them all. The Bristol K type is probably most symbolic of company vehicles, bridging the gap between the linear designs of the pre-war years with the more curvy manifestations of the post-war era. Among preservationists, Graham Ledger from Northants deserves much praise for his exceptional Bristol KSG. He said:

Main UCOC Works superintendent, Bill Horwood, in white smock, poses with body shop staff and one of four VRTs the company had painted in their original red, white and blue livery, for the sixtieth Jubilee year celebration – registration HBD165N. The chosen VRs were from Kettering, Northampton, Wellingborough and Milton Keynes. (Bill Horwood)

Hunsbury Hill Industrial Museum, Northampton, held an open day on Saturday 13 September 1981 and invited enthusiasts to attend. UCOC, always an enthusiast's company, were celebrating their Diamond Jubilee. They sent VR HRP674N, number 834 to the gathering, seen here to the left of Northampton Corporation Transport's 250 Daimler CV6G with Roe bodywork. On the far right we glimpse an ex-London Transport Merlin. (Andrew Shouler)

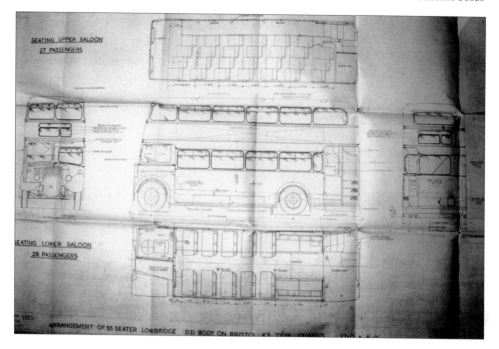

Eastern Coachwork plans for the UCOC and general Tilling stalwart, Bristol K type. The K type chassis was unveiled at the first ever Commercial Motor Show to be held at Earls Court, along with the L type single-deck equivalent. The first Ks were K5Gs, the number denoting engine cylinders and the G being for Gardner engines – petrol engines were no longer fitted to Bristols. The plan shows staggered ECW seating, for ease of access and fare collection from the dropped passenger way – which allowed low bridge bus body height. (Bill Horwood)

It was the last of the seven foot six inch wide K by a long way and was new in 1950. Everything went to a dealer. Outsiders had no chance of buying direct when the buses were scrapped. I bought mine off Sid Twell in Lincolnshire. I remember his house had a lot of trinkets in it. It was the biggest house in the village.

I couldn't drive so I had to persuade a bus driver to bring it back. Being under 20 I wasn't allowed to drive it. When I did learn, by hiring vans, I made a lot of mistakes with the crash gearbox. It was in good condition when I bought it, but I started major restoration work in 2000. All the body panelling is new. The company logo was made from a tracing. I gave the tracing to a vinyl firm and paid £30 for 20. I have never kept a record of the cost of keeping the bus over the last 35 years.

I bought it for preservation in the first place because, I think, when you are young you don't like change. As you get older you don't care because there are too many other things to think about. My bus is a monument to the craftsmanship of Bridlington and Lowestoft. The bus provides a marker along the line of progress in bus development.

Tilling were obsessed with costing; after each day a lot of their female clerks worked out each vehicle's fuel consumption. Drivers would have to account for big discrepancies. If they had gone the way of London Transport with pre selector gear boxes, life would have been easier for the drivers but not for fuel consumption. Bristols were more economic.

PRIVATE HIRE SERVICE

WE WILL —

★ SUBMIT QUOTATIONS TO SUIT THE INDIVI-
   DUAL REQUIREMENTS OF YOUR PARTY

★ PROVIDE NEW SUPER-LUXURY COACHES

★ SUGGEST ATTRACTIVE ITINERARIES AND
   PLACES OF INTEREST AND AMUSEMENT IF
   DESIRED

★ BOOK SEATS FOR THEATRES, PANTOMIME,
   SPORTING EVENTS, etc.

★ RELIEVE YOU OF ANXIETY AS TO YOUR
   TRAVEL ARRANGEMENTS

OUR LONG EXPERIENCE IN CATERING FOR PRIVATE
PARTY TRAVEL IS AT YOUR DISPOSAL, AND WILL HELP
TO MAKE YOUR OUTING A PLEASANT EXPERIENCE AND
A SUCCESS

An idyllic image from an early post-war company Touring advertisement. (Colin Harvey Taylor)

UCOC number 837 stands at Derngate bus station, Northampton on 15 March 1973. This bus
was formerly Luton Corporation Transport's 177 and passed to UCOC (along with seventy-six
fellow vehicles) when they took over Luton Corporation Transport in January 1970. Registered as
177HTM, it was an Albion, with Leyland 9.8 litre diesel engine and sixty-five-seater Neepsend sixty-
five-seater body. Neepsend was a John Brown Engineering group company and this was built to East
Lancs design. (Andrew Shouler)

Lodekka number 654 photographed at Bedford bus station on 5 March 1972. The bus was working a
service to Luton via Ampthill and carries a distinctive advert for Royal Blue Express Coach services.
(Andrew Shouler)

Above: Photographed on Sunday 18 March 1973 at the Central workshops in Houghton Road, Northampton, courtesy of the District Engineer, RE number 263 stands with her nose uncovered, while being re-wired due to an electrical short behind the windscreen. The engineer explained that this class were very susceptible to shorts and burnouts – it took three weeks to completely re-wire one vehicle, including removing/replacing of the trim panels. (Andrew Shouler)

Above: Ex-Southern Vectis Bedford SB Duple Vega coach seen just after leaving Derngate bus station and heading to Hanslope village in north Bucks, beyond Salcey Forest. (Andrew Shouler)

Opposite below: One of eight Eastern National coach seat FLFs hired to fill the breach during a period when high passenger demand, through regional population growth and new bus shortages, caused problems. This picture was taken on 25 May 1973, in Marefair and the ENOC FLF is working route 321. (Andrew Shouler)

As part of a major group, some interesting vehicle transfers took place, including the appearance of two completely non-standard Bedford SB/Duple Vega forty-one-seater coaches, bought from Southern Vectis, a fellow Tilling company on the Isle of Wight in December 1967 when they were about ten years old. Number 112 was allocated to Kettering and 113 to Northampton. Bedford were a popular choice for independents across the country and the SBs were popular with UCOC crews. UCOC were faced with a problem in 1973. Their route mileage was increasing with the growth of the 'new towns' in their area: Milton Keynes, Northampton, Corby etc. Due to various industrial problems of the decade, delivery of buses on order was delayed. In an effort to ease the situation, UCOC purchased many second-hand vehicles and hired others from adjacent operators. Their long-standing relationship with Eastern National allowed for eight coach seated FLFs coming in to temporary service. They had only sixteen seats downstairs, with a large luggage room at the rear and thirty-seven seats upstairs.

Among those buses that we miss, there were many variations, but generally it is the well-balanced design of Bristol chassis harmonised with ECW bodies that was the hallmark of the Tilling era. In the early 1970s, there was still quite an age range of design, from the Ks,

Eastern Scottish VRT, new in 1968, stands in UCOC's Northampton backyard in March 1973. It had been exchanged for UCOC 736, a 1967 FLF6B Lodekka. However, UCOC's depot engineer, himself a Scotsman, said at the time that this VRT 'was no good' and it was being sent back north of the border. (Andrew Shouler)

This UCOC RE has a visitor at lunchtime, for company at the Northampton depot, in the form of a Southdown coach wearing its distinctive light and dark green livery. The vehicle, a Leopard with Duple coach work, was working an extended tour up from Brighton on 5 April 1973 and had disgorged passengers to the Grand Hotel in Gold Street. (Andrew Shouler)

Derngate, Sunday morning, 5 January 1975, a Leyland National and two Bedford YRT/Willowbrooks fifty-three-seat buses are waiting on the stands. The lightweight YRTs had a short life by UCOC standards, all being withdrawn by September 1981. (Andrew Shouler)

to the REs and the interloper Leyland Nationals, all running alongside. Most passengers probably never noticed the old models disappear and the new ones arrive. To them they were just buses, though they would notice the difference if a K type turned up to carry them in to work or town now. That's because, over the years, the progress in design, comfort and safety has been considerable. There can be no return to the good old days. Such was the excellence of the Bristol VR, however, that many are still in service in parts of Britain and the model set the standard for future designs. No doubt if Leyland had not sealed their fate, Bristol would have gone on to greater things, but sadly their last chassis carried the Leyland badge instead of theirs (Devon General's 1814 – registration A686 KDV).

Maybe it is a fitting turn for the Leyland name to have resurfaced in those final days of Tilling style UCOC, going full circle to the type of the bus with which the intrepid two moonlighter busmen founded the illustrious United Counties Omnibus Co. Modern liveries may be stylish, but there was something terribly rural, reassuring and sedate about the UCOC green bus taking its time along the highways and by ways. Even the timetables were colourful and took time and space to inform you of all sorts of things, apart from the time of the buses. For example they listed early closing and market days throughout their service area and notified the running of special hospital buses. Early closing was a quaint custom and a thing of a bygone and less money-mad age. The timetable also listed the populations of all the company's major destinations and places along the way. There were lists of all the parcel agents too.

Taken at lunchtime on Thursday 8 February 1973, a handsome KSW, JBD965, new in 1953, was one of the few remaining K types in service at that time. Here it is resting in the autumn of its existence and soon to be growling up to hill top Duston Village on the 322. It is easy to see where the Revd Awdry got his inspiration from, for one could easily imagine sullen looks coming from the REs standing alongside. (Andrew Shouler)

An array of regulations and conditions pertaining to passengers and parcels were also spelled out in some detail in the 1965 timetable. For example:

(12) The passenger is further carried subject to the provisions of Statutory Instrument No. 1612, 1954 the purpose of which is as follows:

The number of passengers to be carried on a vehicle shall not exceed the ascertained seating capacity except that in the case of a stage carriage or an express carriage carrying conductor additional passengers not exceeding one third of the number of passengers for which the vehicle, or in the case of a doubledecked vehicle the lower deck, has seating capacity to, or eight, whichever number is the less, may be carried.

No standing passengers will be carried (a) on the upper deck of a double deck vehicle, (b) if there is any vacant seat in the vehicle.

Standing passsengers are not permitted to travel on the platform or staircase of a double decked vehicle or on the steps of a single deck vehicle or standing against the emergency exit door or doors.

Passengers are carried at the absolute discretion of the company whose decision and that of its emloyees is absolute.

Above is but one extract from five tightly packed pages of small print rules and regulations from what had become a complex and risk laden business. The rules stated that 'Parcels are conveyed to and from any place along the routes served by the Company's PSVs.

Every effort will be made to ensure prompt delivery to consignees (who will sign for same on delivery) meeting the PSV at conignor's risk, and will be accepted from consignors at the consignor's risk. The Company accepts no responsibility for loss or damage, howsoever the same may be caused…' With conditions like that, one might be surprised anyone ever sent a parcel by UCOC. Nearly two whole pages of rules were devoted to the conduct of passengers, starting reasonably with the rule that passengers or intending passengers shall not: 'Use obscene or offensive language or conduct himself in a riotous or disorderly manner'. The rules then get more exotic: 'Enter or alight from the vehicle otherwise than by the doors or openings provided for the purpose. When entering or attempting to enter the vehicle wilfully and unreasonably impede passengers seeking to enter the vehicle or to alight therefrom.'

The above is but an small extract. There is also advice concerning queues, including the phrase: 'A person must not enter or endeavour to enter a vehicle when it is approaching and or about to stop at a stopping place before any other person desiring to enter that vehicle who was waiting in a queue or line at that stopping place.' Another interesting reference under passengers, reads: 'In certain areas of the Company and on certain services at specified times, by authorisation of the Licensing Authority, a form of priority is in operation giving precedence to certain classes of passengers in such circumstances who are not included in such classes.' All this sounds rather quaint, as do references to lost property: 'Any person who finds property accidentally left in a vehicle shall immediately hand it in the state in which he finds it to the Conductor ("Conductor" includes Driver where no Conductor is carried on the vehicle) who shall deal with it in accordance with these regulations…'.

In the leaner, fitter Thatcher years, the long, winding 346 route could not exist. Driver Walter 'Foggy' Warwick described the route as 'a good steady run'. His colleague Ray Fall was equally enthusiastic, saying:

> I'd rather go on something like the 346, it was the longest route. We used to look after the passengers. If we knew they lived in an isolated village and travelled, we'd wait until they got there. We had plenty of time when we got to Aylesbury. I liked to browse in Weatherhead's bookshop on Kingsbury Square, where the bus station was until the late 1960s. I liked the market as well.

Driver Brian Dale, who left Stagecoach in 2005, summed up the changes: 'The bus company used to be people focused, but it is now time focused'.

Back in 1972, service 346 was a convenient two-hour journey, now nearly thirty-five years later it can take much longer because there is no direct route and a Stagecoach X4 from Northampton to Milton Keynes takes forty-five minutes. Then there is a thirty-five minute wait for Arriva X15 to Aylesbury, via Leighton Buzzard, takes eighty minutes – and if you want any of the villages between Aylesbury and Buckingham you have to catch the 66 back in the direction of Northampton.

Margaret Thatcher came to power on the back of trade union unrest unprecedented since unions began in the nineteenth centrury. Her Government had given clear signals

Above: Photographed in Houghton Road, Northampton on 31 May 1973, here are two new VRTs already allocated to Luton and waiting to trundle down the M1 to their depot. (Andrew Shouler)

Left: Lodekka 547 sedately proceeds down Stony Stratford's High Street back to its Northampton base. At that time the A5 Watling Street was a busy thoroughfare straight through the town centre, until Milton Keynes expansion brought the A5D relief road. This bus was an LD6B, new in 1958. (Andrew Shouler)

This AEC Matador was number 80 in the service fleet. New in 1950, it was the tractor unit of an articulated lorry owned by a Lincoln transport contarctor. Bought by UCOC in 1968, it was converetd in their workshop to a recovery vehicle and was withdrawn in December 1974. It is seen here in Northampton, wearing trade plates prior to disposal (Andrew Shouler)

It looks like there is a bit of speed on RE number 313 as it crosses the reverse camber entering Victoria Promenade from Derngate, Northampton, on the 332 to Horton on 1 July 1974 at 1.10 p.m. New in 1968, it carries a patchwork paint of UCOC Tilling and National Bus apple greens. Following behind is Bedford 101, new in that year, with Willowbrook bus body seating fifty-three and working the 326 north to Guilsborough and Market Harborough. (Andrew Shouler)

A very 1970s scene at Bedford bus station on Saturday 3 March 1972 at 3.30 p.m. Bus and multi-storey car parks offer a timely contrast between modest little bus station buildings and the overwhelming multi-storey car park, home to the overwhelming motor cars. The image also makes a contrast in OMO loadings. Furthest from camera is 207, a Duple-bodied RELH on the 15.30 service to Bromham, whilst closer to view is 139, an MW re-seated to forty-five bus seats on service 157 to Wootton at 15.35. The well-behaved girls, after attending Saturday morning school in their smart Dame Alice School uniforms, have taken advanatage of some time to buy shopping before heading home. (Andrew Shouler)

Taken during the eveining of Tuesday 19 April 1973, RE number 263 cools off on Newport Pagnell Market Hill, having left Victoria at 5.30 p.m. on the X6. It has another 15 miles of its journey left to its Northampton destination. (Andrew Shouler)

Stoke Goldington, as shown at the beginning of this book, was on the old Royal Mail coach routes and its express coaches have continued to pass through the pretty village for years since. Here we see UCOC RE 254 passing through on Sunday 13 July 1975, working a duplicate to Luton Airport. The service car was MW coach 261, which would work on through to Victoria and had just passed through. Number 254 is in full National Coach livery, as were sisters 258 and 259, but Rushden's allocation 251 was in local coach livery of white and apple green. The usual duplicate vehicle used that summer was ex-Court Line Ford/Elite also in local coach livery. The rockery being constructed in the background is on the site of the original Wesley's Coach services garage. (Andrew Shouler)

An MW, number 261, thirty-nine-seat coach leads RELH/DP49F, number 210 on the 18.00 X6 service to Victoria, Stoke Goldington High Street, 28 August 1972. (Andrew Shouler)

Houghton Road depot, Northampton, 26 September 1974, and we see bodywork contrasts, but under their skins these buses were the same, both RELHs. On the right we have RELH number 266, new in 1967 and just in off the 555 Victoria–Northampton. By the garage wall, we see number 219 with Plaxton Elite Express III coach body, seating forty-nine and new in May 1974, some four months before the picture was taken, and in off the Bristol service 746, arriving into Northampton at 12.30 p.m. – just thirty minutes before the photograph was taken. (Andrew Shouler)

Departing Derngate bus station, Northampton, and heading back to its Aylesbury base at 15.00, is number 773, registration ANV 773J, a VRTSL6G with seventy-seater ECW body and the original flat front. This bus had left Aylesbury at 12.48 and after heading north through Winslow, Buckigham and Towcester, had arrived at 2.44. (Andrew Shouler)

Pictured at 1.30 p.m. on Wednesday 10 September 1980, UCOC's National Express 273, an RELH6G with DP47 seats, waits in Victoria Street due to Greyfriars pickets. This bus was new in April 1968, passing to a dealer in December 1982. It carried a variety of liveries – starting with UCOC cream and green, then National Express all over white, then National Bus white over apple green, when it was allocated to Luton. Finally it reverted to full National livery and was allocated back to Northampton in July 1980 – as seen here. (Andrew Shouler)

that they were going to do something about it. Managers in both the public and private sector could expect as much. Some would argue that the Tories of this period went out of their way to provoke trouble. It was also the era when computers came of age and there was great faith in the new service economy.

Industry would become leaner and fitter. In other words there would be fewer factory workers to ride buses to work. Employees of UCOC, like many others, feared for their security of employment under an increasingly strident Government, who's employment secretary, Jim Prior, was warning of record levels of unemployment in the new age economy where manufacturing was increasingly diverting to the Third World. Not surprisingly UCOC employees became embroiled in industrial protest.

As a result of a UCOC strike from 31 August to 20 September 1980 over the manning of revised schedules, Greyfriars bus station, Northampton, was closed to National Express and Northampton Corporation Transport, by pickets. Consequently, National Express, Premier Travel and Yelloway used Campbell Square and Victoria Street. No amount of industrial action, however, was going to turn the clock back as a whole raft of legislation quickly emascualted the unions.

Brian Dale learned to drive a bus in 1970, whilst full-time at London Brick Co. and part-time for Paynes and Langstone and Tasker. Those were the days when you could take an empty coach out by yourself to get the hang of it. Paynes lent him the coach. He passed second time because the first time the examiner spotted a cracked

Alexander-bodied Leopard, MRP225P, from Milton Keynes allocation, photographed in August 1982, with the 12.20 p.m. at Heathrow central bus station. This bus could cruise at 75mph, comfortably in pre-limiter days. (Andrew Shouler)

Above: Greyfriars bus station, 1 June 1981 and number 248, an Elite III-bodied Leyland Leopard bears the Nottingham destination on its route blind. This bus had a varied lifespan. New in March 1971, being bought from National Travel West in November 1981, it was soon withdrawn. Brand new number 150, Willowbrook Leopard forty-seven-seater stands just behind – it was sold to Milton Keynes City Bus in January 1986. (Andrew Shouler)

Opposite: United Counties Stage Carriage Services 1953. (Colin Harvey Taylor)

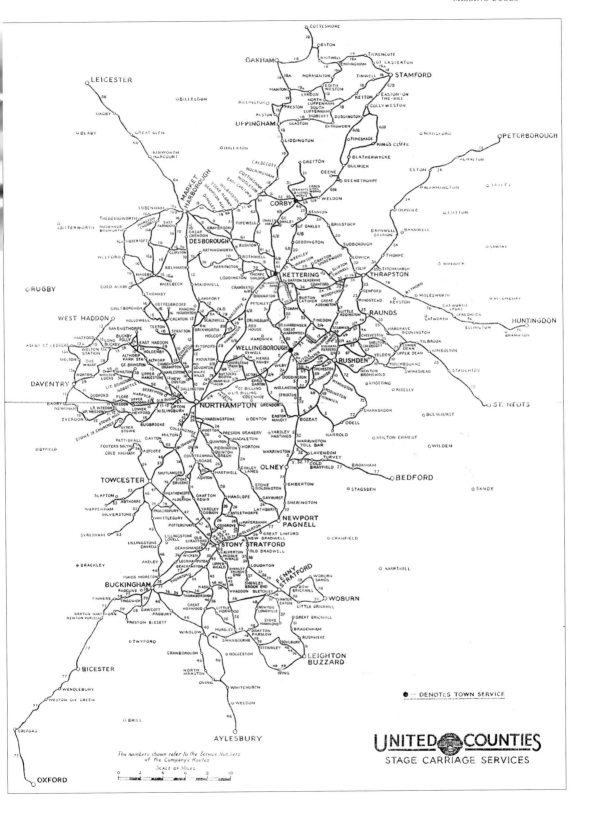

About to turn from Derngate into Victoria Promenade is Northampton's 302, bound for Daventry on country village route 305. This bus was one of six lightweight SU Bristol chassis with thirty-six seats – a simple effective vehicle for country routes. Complete, it cost less than £4,000. New in May 1966, they were withdrawn in late 1974. A Royal Blue Coach hurries up from the UCOC depot to the bus station to the south west. (R.H.G. Simpson)

Photographed on the Isle of Wight, in August 2002, is a partially restored ex-UCOC Bristol SC4LK, registration ONV425, with ECW thirty-five-seat bus body. It was one of five bought in 1957 for OMO use and sold on to Red & White MS and Cumberland MS in 1962. This one ended up on the Isle of Wight, where it was photogarphed near Ryde, and was ideally suited to the island's narrow lanes. (Robert Cook)

indicator lense and wouldn't let him pop into the UCOC garage in Tavistock Street to borrow a screwdriver and new lense. Then came a spell with UCOC in 1970. When the brickworks closed down, his skills were much in demand at Stagecoach UCOC and he went straight in as a driver.

Brian explained how many of the rural diversions to routes disappeared because people needed to go faster and much of the village locality was eroded. He started in 1991 at the company's Silverstone outstation, where there was one bus and three home based crews. He drove the Northampton–Oxford route through Milton Malsor, Blisworth, the Towcester loop and on to Whittlebury, Silverstone, Syresham, Brackley, Evenley, Fringford, Stratton Audley, Bicester, Wendlebury, Weston on the Green, Bletchington and Kiddlington. He also drove the intermediate direct route between the same destinations.

Over time people needed to get places so much more quickly and in his final years, the only pick up and set down points were at Towcester, Brackley and Bicester, with B10Ms taking over the route, or the low floor single-deckers. He talked of a changing culture, as so many others have done:

Now everybody has become a number, not an individual. De-regulation was inevitable. Today's environment is so different, people look for a lot more in their transport. There has to be a forward movement in public transport because there just isn't the road facility to take the traffic.

I have always been in and around transport. I have done the job over the years with a lot of interest and will always do it to the best of my ability. Unfortunately a driver's responsibilities are still not reflected in the rate of pay, though it was better when I left United Counties in 2005 than when I started, almost doubling from £4.50 an hour to £8.00. Originally I worked 47 hours a week, then in latter days the 39 hour standard.

One-man bus operation makes a driver more vulnerable. Conductors would help you turn the bus around on a dark night in the countryside. You helped each other. There's better lighting and no really remote locations. People can create difficulties, but a lot of that can be tempered by attitudes.

These days there's an emphasis on qualifications and everybody will have to be NVQ qualified by 2008-9. Some traditions prevail. Inspectors tend to come from the older element, though there is a young offroad inspector with around 5 years experience of the industry. He looks after the allocation of work, vehicles, and duty rosters. Strikes don't happen because there is a necessity for people to be more committed to the job. This is because they have to take account of what's going on in the outside world. People have higher living standards and expenses.

The modern bus company is run by a new breed, though Brian Dale recalls that some old hands are still working at UCOC, men like depot manager Rod Davies who, he says, knew the job inside out. Brian also praises Howard Butler in operations at Rothersthorpe Road, as a man who is a good people person, knowing how to get the best out of the busmen and a keen preservationist. Fred Newman is another who respected manager Rod Davies for taking the express coaches out himself, though Brian Dale observed that managerial promotion these days has much to do with the embracing of new technology than the bus driver's steering wheel. Fred Newman reminisced:

> In the old days they gave you route learning, following the service coach in a duplicate and you found your own way back. They said you learn quicker in the driving seat. It was a big change leaving Derngate for Greyfriars, a cold place, even in summer. It was built on a graveyard. By the end of the old United Counties we were no longer the elite. My earliest shift was 6am going out, two hours to Victoria, or three hours off the motorway, via Newport Pagnell, Stoke Goldington, Luton and St Albans. Going out of London on the motorway service you didn't pick anyone up after Hendon. I left and went back some years later. It wasn't the same. National Express changed things, United Counties gave a lot of the express work away.

Some might say that the powers that were in charge of de-regulation gave an awful lot more away. However, that was the bus world that was — or at least a partial view. Whatever the spin doctors might like to tell the gullible, the old world had its virtues, but it was the people of that world that made the present. One thing has led to another and the past was far from perfect. To us, nonetheless, we feel that technology is being used to benefit a minority and for the sake of short-term profit. We have sympathy for the busmen of the 1930s who saw the danger of becoming part of the Tilling empire. Most of us are subjects of empire builders large and small and we should question that.

All we have is the present to deal with and our memories to cherish or to learn from. For those who love a rambling bus ride there are still some windy routes to enjoy, like service 24 to Bedford via Central Milton Keynes, Newport Pagnell, Sherington and the main road villages of Chichley, Astwood, Stagsden and Bromham — one and a half hours of sheer delight. Generally though, the frequency and diversity of routes is not there and tickets are expensive on sometimes almost empty vehicles. In spite of privatisation, the future of public transport is still in the hands of politicians. In the meantime, there is no harm in looking back at the old world, through rose-tinted spectacles, at the buses we miss.

De-regulation was half a decade away when this picture was taken in December 1980. The buses look good on bleak Beltchely bus station and services were already in decline through lack of demand and staff shortage. Bristol VRIII, 905, stands in the foreground in City Bus livery. (Andrew Shouler)

On the rural trail, number 150 accelerates downhill through wooded North Bucks before entering Stoke Goldington. (Andrew Shouler)

Left: Since joining Eastern National, busman John Payne had nearly done it all, except join management. When this picture was taken in the 1970s, the last full decade of United Counties, at the company's Aylesbury depot, he had become a fitter. He is seen here, with his assistant, working on an unidentified VR. (*Bucks Herald*)

Below: A great deal of National Bus real estate became expensive new town centre housing. This sedate example of Tilling brick work, in Aylesbury's Buckingham Road, was flourishing when this picture was taken in the late 1960s. After passing to Luton & District, who then re-located to an industrial estate, the redundant depot suffered the indignity of life as a temporary NCP car park before redevelopement for homes. (R.H.G. Simpson)

A pristine perserved FS Lodekka, 712, attending a springtime rally at Quainton Railway Centre near Aylesbury. New in 1966, it was withdrawn in August 1981 and passed to D. Riley at Luton the following month. Beautifully cared for, the fleet number is displayed in the route box, under its home town name. The bus also carries a Luton allocation plate. (Nicola Cook)

Where it all began with Tilling and other major pioneers, a Routemaster (RML2286 reg CUV286C) on London's Route 15, in the West End, September 1999. The bus was then in the same ownership as the rump of United Counties. The famous Stagecoach legend is (East London) emblazened in gold on the side. (Robert Cook)

Above: RM 682, photographed at a PSV gathering on Northampton Market Square in 1998. The bus was new to London Transport in April 1961. Originally regsitered as WLT682, it was re-registered HVS937 and is dressed in the livery of Stagecoach United Counties, showing Bedford Town service 106 to Harrowden Road. It features informative LT-style blinds and is parked in front of UCOC

VRT number 962 – registration VVV962W – which carried a seventy-four-seat ECW body and was new in April 1981. The VRT was repainted into Coachlinks livery and then back into standard Stagecoach style. The X94 service was Northampton, Wellingborough, Rushden, Thrapston and Oundle to Peterborough. Its sister route X65 (joint with Cambus) traversed the Northamptonshire heights, via Kettering and Corby, before dropping down to the river Nene at Oundle, to Peterborough. (Robert Cook)

Left: Graham Ledger with his preserved 1950 Bristol KS6G in April 2006. He bought the vehicle from a dealer in Lincoln for £80 in 1970, having found it impossible to buy directly from UCOC. (Robert Cook)

Almost where it all began, a tranquil market town scene and a sturdy little Lodekka trundles away from Derngate, en route to Moulton in the early 1960s. This is the sort of UCOC image that many of us love to remember. (John Royle)

As much as some of us may admire the buses, the whole enterprise would not have worked without people, like Ray Fall pictured here in the late 1960s at Derngate. Buses were and still are about people. (Ray Fall)

217

Above: Some of the old faces from Northampton UCOC days, pictured here at a reunion in the 1980s. The front row are, left to right: Shirley Coleman, Mrs Nightingale, -?-, George Egan, Fred Amos and Norman Maycock – standing. Second row, left to right: Bill Meredith, Peter Pachesa, Wilf Billingham, Reg Cox, and Agnes Smith. Third row, left to right: Bernard Reeve, Ray Fall, Doug Belgrove, -?-, and Peter Clack. Back row, left to right: Mary Solomon, W Reford, -?-, Albert Houghton. (Ray Fall)

Left: Romance on the buses was not unkown, though perhaps not as wild as the television image of *On the Buses* would have us believe. This is Mr and Mrs Fred Newman in the 1950s, when they both worked for Northampton Corporation. Fred soon transferred his services to the more wide-roaming United Counties. (Fred Newman)

Probably fitter Les Colman's most embarrassing moment on the buses, May 1964. After collecting this KSW from Derngate, he is believed to have clipped the kerb and lost his grip on the steering wheel, causing the bus to mount the pavement and become perilously wedged under a canopy. Steering on these vehicles was heavy, especially when a second tread had been cut in the tyres. (W.J.S. Meredith)

A typical 1960s scene during the old UCOC's twilight years, as Lodekka number 712 enters Stony Stratford bus station on 25 March 1967. (John Royle)

Another idyllic UCOC scene, with Lodekka number 956 in Wolverton Road, Stony Stratford. These were the days of proper buses, we think. We miss them. (John Royle)

INDEX

If you are interested in purchasing other books published by Tempus,
or in case you have difficulty finding any Tempus books in your local bookshop,
you can also place orders directly through our website

www.tempus-publishing.com